Using
The
OXFORD

DICTIONARY

John Butterworth

Illustrated by Kate Sheppard

Oxford University Press

Oxford University Press, Walton Street, Oxford OX2 6DP

Oxford   New York   Toronto
Delhi   Bombay   Calcutta   Madras   Karachi
Kuala Lumpur   Singapore   Hong Kong   Tokyo
Nairobi   Dar es Salaam   Cape Town
Melbourne   Auckland   Madrid

and associated companies in
Berlin   Ibadan

Oxford is a trade mark of Oxford University Press

Text copyright © **John Butterworth 1994**
Illustrations copyright © **Kate Sheppard 1994**

First published 1994
3 5 7 9 10 8 6 4 2

British Library Cataloguing in Publication Data
Data available
ISBN 0 19 910307 0 (paperback)
Printed in Great Britain

OWLS
OXFORD ENGLISH
DICTIONARY
WORD AND
LANGUAGE
SERVICE

Do you have a query about words, their origin, meaning, use, spelling,
pronunciation, or any other aspect of the English language? Then write to
OWLS at Oxford University Press, Walton Street, Oxford OX2 6DP.

All queries will be answered using the full resources of the
Oxford Dictionary Department.

Contents

Introduction

This is a book of activities and games to be used alongside *The Oxford Primary School Dictionary*. It will help you to understand dictionaries and to get the most out of them.

You can find a great wealth of information in a dictionary, if you know how to use it. But unless you are familiar with the way a dictionary works, it can seem more like a maze than a useful and helpful reference book. *Using the Oxford Primary School Dictionary* is a guide to help you explore the dictionary and to find your way around it.

The book divides into two parts. The activities in *Part One* give you practice at finding words and making sense of what the dictionary says about them. You will learn about the different kinds of English words, what they can do, and what they mean. You will also discover how words change to suit their different uses, and when it is right to use some words and wrong to use others.

Part Two consists of *Puzzle Pages*: quizzes and games where the answers are hidden in the dictionary, or where the dictionary is the 'referee'. Many of these are cross-curricular, which means that they belong not just to English, but to mathematics, music, geography, history, technology and science. And there are others based on everyday activities such as shopping, travelling and solving problems.

The tasks in both parts of the book are fun to do, which is important, because language should be fun. Some may seem fairly easy; others will be challenging and puzzling. Enjoy them and do them well, and they will show you what a varied and fascinating book the dictionary is.

Dictionary features

A dictionary contains words that are used in a language. *The Oxford Primary School Dictionary* is an English language dictionary that is full of information about words and the way we use them.

What can you find out from the dictionary? Use your copy to answer the questions in the quiz.

A How many letters are there in the alphabet?

Write them down in order.

B Look up the word **dictionary**. What are the two most important uses of a dictionary?

C What are some other uses of a dictionary? It will help if you look at the pages in the front and at the back of the dictionary.

All in order

To help you find words in the dictionary, they are in alphabetical order.

A See how quickly you can find the following words. Time yourself.

tennis
volleyball
athletics
football
chess

B Can you find these in the dictionary?

1 a *fish* and a *bird* that begin with **her**

2 a unit of *time*, a unit of *length*, and a unit of *money* that all begin with **y**

3 a *motor vehicle* and a *boat* that begin with **tra**

Use the dictionary to find six animals beginning with the letter **p**, and write them down in alphabetical order. Don't forget that 'animals' include birds, fish and insects.

C Put the following musical instruments into the order they come in the dictionary:

flute
trumpet
piano
guitar
violin
cello
drum

D   Sort these animals into alphabetical order:

>   **butterfly**
>   **boxer**
>   **bird**
>   **bat**
>   **bear**
>   **bloodhound**

E   These words all begin with the same **two** letters. Put them into alphabetical order:

>   **digger**
>   **dimmer**
>   **differ**
>   **dither**
>   **diver**

F   Rewrite these words in alphabetical order:

>   **Mad mechanic Mick made monstrous mistakes mending motors.**

Can you think of a silly sentence in which all the words begin with the same letter? Use the dictionary to help you.

Guides

To make it easier to find a word, most dictionaries have **guide** words at the top of their pages. In *The Oxford Primary School Dictionary*, they tell you the *first* and *last* words on the double page.

A Look up the word **spot**. What two guide words does it come between?

Do the same for these words:

stair
roof
ceiling

B Use the guide words to help you look up the names of these birds:

hawk
sparrow
swallow

C These are two guide words from the dictionary:

stutter	430	431	**suffocate**

Can you think of six or more words that would be on these two pages?

Write them down.

Find these two guide words in *The Oxford Primary School Dictionary* and see how many words you could have written.

Squeeze

This is a game for two or more players and a referee who has the dictionary.

The referee chooses a double page from the dictionary and tells the players the guide words. For example:

firework 164	165 **flash**^{2}

Players (or teams) must give words which come between the guides. If you get one wrong, or you can't think of a word at all, you miss a turn.

Keep the score (one point for each word – write them down). No points for repeating the same words! When no one can think of any more words to squeeze in, the game ends. The winner is the player or team with the most words.

Pick a new referee and start again.

Entries

Each of the short sections in a dictionary is called an **entry**.

The entry begins with the **headword** in bold letters. The rest of the entry gives you information about the headword or words related to it.

A Not all dictionary entries are the same length. Take the headwords:

brag and **break**

Try to guess which will have the bigger entry. Then look them up and see if you were right.

Can you see any other ways in which the two entries are different? For instance, which one has example sentences showing how the word is used?

B Look carefully at several different entries in your dictionary. Do you notice any kinds of information that *all* the entries have? List them.

C Here is a dictionary entry for the word **king**:

> **king** *noun* (**kings**)
> **1** a man who has been crowned as the ruler of a country. **2** a piece in chess. **3** a playing card with a picture of a king on it.
> **kingly** *adjective*

Can you explain why there are numbers in the entry?

D Write an entry for the word **queen** using numbers for different parts of the entry. Then compare your entry with the one for **queen** in the dictionary.

E Sometimes the headwords themselves have numbers after them:

> **bat**¹ *noun* (**bats**)
>   a wooden implement used to hit the ball in
>   cricket, baseball, and other games
>
> **bat**² *noun* (**bats**)
>   a flying mammal that looks like a mouse with
>   wings

Why do you think there is more than one entry for the word **bat**?

What's the meaning?

The main job of a dictionary is to tell us what words mean and to show us how they are spelt.

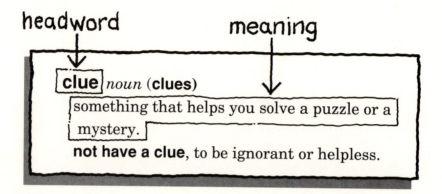

A How would you explain the meanings of the words:

solve
puzzle
mystery

Compare your answers with the meanings given in the dictionary.

B Complete the headwords that have these meanings:

1 **pr** _ _ _ _ _   something difficult to answer, understand, or overcome.

2 **tr** _ _ _   something done to deceive or fool someone.

3 **ri** _ _ _ _   a puzzling question, especially as a joke

4 **so** _ _ _ _ _ _   the answer to a problem or puzzle.

5 **per** _ _ _ _   to puzzle someone very much.

6 **sur** _ _ _ _ _   something that you did not expect.

7 **sus** _ _ _ _ _   an anxious or uncertain feeling while waiting for an event, information etc.

C Fill in the missing words, or parts of words, in the sentences below.

(You can use *The Oxford Primary School Dictionary* to help.)

1 If you want a bike to run smoothly, you need to
lu _ _ _ _ _ _ **e** it.

2 Deserts are **ar** _ _ places.

3 The way into the hotel is through the **fo** _ **er**.

4 Nothing was **sal** _ _ _ _ **d** from the shipwreck.

5 The number of spectators **dw** _ _ _ _ _ **d** to less than a dozen.

6 Detectives have to be **perc** _ _ _ _ _ _ in spotting clues.

7 A huge earthquake registered on the **sei** _ _ _ _ _ _ _ _ .

8 You can make your pocket money last longer by being more
ec _ _ _ _ _ _ **al** with it.

9 The **d** _ _ _ _ _ diagnosed a rare, tropical disease.

10 Sun, wind and water are forms of renewable _ _ _ _ _ _ .

Alike – but different

Some words have very similar **meanings**. You can use a dictionary to discover how they differ.

A   Say how the words in each box are alike. Then say what is different about each one.

> hill   mountain   peak   fell

> river   stream   canal   delta

> street   path   road   lane

> country   county   province   district

> fear   fright   terror   horror

B   Some words are easier to understand if you give an **example** of the way they are used:

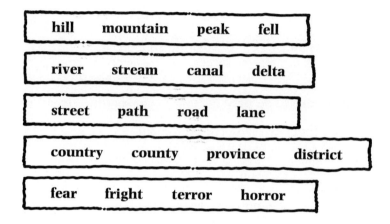

> **growl²** *verb* (**growls, growling, growled**)
> to make a deep, rough sound, *Angry dogs growl.*

In the entry for **growl**, which is the *meaning* and which is the *example*?

How does the dictionary show which is which?

C Think of a short example of the way these words are used:

snort   whine   roar   croak   bellow

Afterwards, look to see if your dictionary gives examples for any of these words.

D You can often tell what a word means just from the words around it in a sentence - even a completely unknown word.

These sentences have been written by a visitor from another planet who is learning English. Every so often he has slipped in a word from his own language.

Eric went to the **klej** of the **griff** and looked down at the sea breaking on the jagged **slocks** below. His mother called to him to take **nare**, but just as she **proke**, the soft earth of the **griff** began to crumble **wax** Eric's feet. He **gan** for safety.

From these clues, what do you think is the meaning of:

klej griff slocks nare proke wax gan

Write dictionary entries for some of them.

Words and pictures

Sometimes the best way to explain the meaning of a word is to show a picture.

A   Write the word *and* the definition that you think belong with each of these pictures.

Compare your answers with the dictionary entries for the words you have written. Were you right?

B Match these words with the pictures below them:

webbed   **gargoyle**   **digital**   **quill**

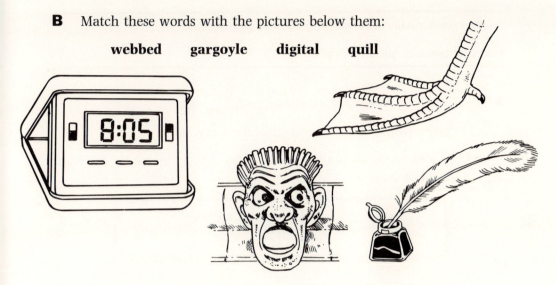

C First, draw a simple picture to illustrate each of these words:

crane   a machine for lifting and moving heavy objects

dustpan   a pan into which dust is brushed from the floor

guitar   a musical instrument with strings that you pluck

nozzle   the part at the end of a hose or pipe from which something flows

buckle   a fastener for a belt or strap

Then check whether the illustrations in *The Oxford Primary School Dictionary* are like yours or very different.

D Look these words up in your dictionary and use the entries to help you draw pictures for them:

gauntlet
mitten
tumbler (meaning 1)
terrace (meaning 1)
convoy

A job to do

'Verb', 'noun', 'adjective', 'adverb', etc. are known as

word classes or **parts of speech.**

A *A heavy lorry **lumbered** slowly up the hill.*

The word **lumbered** tells you what the lorry did.

If you look in the dictionary you will see that the name for this kind of word is a *verb*.

> **lumber**² *verb* (**lumbers, lumbering, lumbered**)
> **1** to move along clumsily or noisily

Look up the words

    lorry   **hill**   **heavy**   **up**   **slowly**

They are not *verbs*. What kinds of word are they?

B Look in the dictionary to see what word class the names for animals are:

    monkey   **bear**   **mongoose**

Make the list ten animals long.

C Find out what part of speech words describing size and shape are:

    long   **tall**   **flat**   **thin**

Think of five or six more to add to the list.

D Here is a list of words that tell how something might move:

quickly   smoothly   awkwardly   backwards

Add a few more. To which word class do these words belong?

E Shaz made an **omelette.**

Shaz made a **mistake.**

Shaz made a ....

Can you think of some more *nouns* for things Shaz might have made?

F Colin **threw** the ball.

Colin **burst** the ball.

Colin .... the ball

What else could Colin have done to the ball? Make as long a list as you can in *one minute.*

What part of speech are the words in your list?

Allsorts

Nouns are words for **things**.

> **thing** *noun* (**things**)
> an object; anything that can be touched,
> seen, thought about, etc.

A Make a list of five things that you can see within a few metres of where you are. Look the words up in the dictionary and see what part of speech they are.

B Look up the words:

{ **woman, boy, sister, mechanic, athlete** }

What are they all words for; and what part of speech are they?

C Here are six more sets of nouns.

1 { **river, mountain, valley, ...** }

2 { **triangle, hexagon, circle, ...** }

3 { **song, ballad, tune, ...** }

4 { **heel, knee, jaw, ...** }

5 { **trawler, schooner, cruiser, ...** }

6 { **bunch, team, crowd, ...** }

Which of the six sets does each of these nouns belong to? Use the dictionary to find out.

**gang   knuckle   square   ocean   verse   yacht
vertebra   galley   ellipse   dinghy   anthem   canyon**

Can you think of one or two more nouns to add to each set?

D These nouns are called **proper nouns,** and they all begin with a capital letter

     James   **Australia**   **Nile**   **Kennedy**   **Paris**

Say what else is different about these nouns, and think of five more examples to add to the list.

Are any of these words in the dictionary, and if so, where?
(Search the back of the dictionary - the part called the *Appendices* - as well as the main part.)

E Nouns which are not **proper nouns** are called **common nouns**.

Complete each of these sentences with a suitable common noun from the list at the end of the exercise.

Asia is a ....

The Amazon is a ....

The Sahara is a ....

Diwali is a ....

Belgium is a ....

     river   **country**   **continent**   **desert**   **festival**

F A **drill** is a particular kind of **tool.**
A **sparrow** is a particular kind of **bird.**

With the help of the dictionary, find a single common noun to complete each of these sentences:

Saris, caftans and **kilts** are all particular kinds of ....

A **kestrel** is a particular type of ....

An **encyclopedia** is one sort of ....

A **saxophone** is a certain kind of musical ....

A **cockroach** is an ....

How much? How many?

A **singular** noun stands for one thing.

A **plural** noun stands for more than one.

> **crocodile** *noun* (**crocodiles**)
> a large reptile living in hot countries,
> with a thick skin, long tail, and huge jaws.

A   Write down the plural form of each of these animals. Check the spelling in the dictionary, if you are unsure.

   ferret   **partridge**   **goose**   **tiger**   **chaffinch**   **fox**

B   The usual rule for making a noun plural is to add **-s** at the end, but this is not always how it is done.

   Can you find the rule for these nouns?

   glass   **dress**   **cross**   **harness**   **bus**

   branch   **bush**   **itch**   **stitch**   **watch**   **crash**

C   These nouns are all plural. Write down their singular forms, and say how they are all alike.

   pennies   **nappies**   **parties**   **cities**   **memories**   **flies**

D   Nouns ending in **-o** are the most difficult to remember.

   Look up the plurals of these to find out why:

   piano   **solo**   **banjo**   **flamingo**   **zoo**

   potato   **tomato**   **volcano**   **mosquito**   **echo**

Most nouns are for things which can be counted (**countable nouns**) but some nouns have no plurals (**uncountable nouns).**

> **coin**[1] *noun* (**coins**)
>   a piece of metal money.

You can say, "One coin, two coins, three coins, four..." **Coin** is a countable noun. But some nouns are uncountable. For example:

> **money** *noun*
>   coins and notes used by people to buy things.

E Why does **money** not have a plural?

Why is it called an uncountable noun?

F Which of these nouns are countable and which are uncountable?

>   **bread** **loaf** **chair** **furniture**
>   **ocean** **water** **fun** **game**

G Think of three more examples of uncountable nouns. Check their entries in the dictionary to see if they have plurals.

H Look up these nouns:

>   **scissors** **trousers** **cattle** **shorts**

What do you notice about them?

I What have the plurals of these nouns got in common?

>   **aircraft** **deer** **sheep**

Describe it

Adjectives are words for describing things.

'There is an animal prowling round the field.'
'Is there? What kind of animal?'
'Well it's ...'

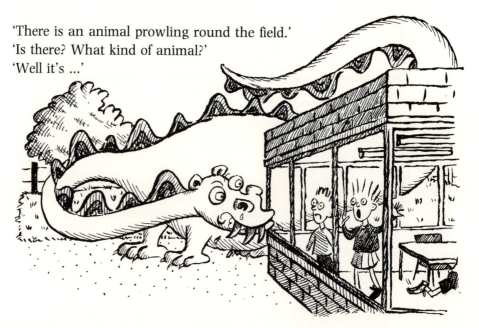

A Which of the following adjectives would you have used to describe the animal on the school field?

> **friendly   dangerous   nasty   grotesque**
>
> **cuddly   timid**

Think of three or four more adjectives which could be used to describe the animal.

You could use each of these adjectives to describe different parts of the animal. Which adjective best describes each part?

> **jagged   ferocious   hefty   cold   flickering**

B From the dictionary, find out something about these animals. Then choose a different adjective to describe each one.

> **eel   lizard   cheetah   sloth   weasel**

Adjectives can be used to **compare** some things with others.

> **cold** *adjective* (**colder, coldest**)
> **1** not hot or warm.

The pool was **cold**.
The sea was **colder**.
The mountain stream was the **coldest** of all.

C Look in the dictionary for help in spelling the different forms. Instead of the word **cold**, use the word **hard** and compare three things. Make up three sentences using the different forms of **sad**.

Write a short paragraph about three boys who get their clothes **dirty**. Who is cleanest and who is most dirty?

D Look up these adjectives in the dictionary:

> **edible**
> **flexible**
> **disposable**
> **inaccessible**

Write down sentences with examples of things which can be described by these adjectives.

Actions

Words that describe actions belong to a large set of words called **verbs.**

Have you ever needed a dictionary in a P.E. or drama lesson? No? Well, now you do.

For the following exercises work in groups of 4-6, with at least one dictionary between you.

A Warm up by performing each of these actions in turn several times:

jump   hop   bound[3]   shake   wobble   slump

B Look up the following verbs in your dictionary.

**lurch   jerk   slouch   flounder   glide   accept
reject   collect   possess   empty**

Choose one of the words and take turns to perform the action. The others in the group have to say which one it is. Use a partner if you need one.

A person (or thing) that *does* something in a sentence is known as the **subject.**

C   Take turns pretending that you are the subject of the following sentences. Act out what the sentence says. Then look at the questions underneath.

1   Julie tiptoed silently away from the door.

2   The animal leapt through the air with a roar.

3   The policeman arrested the burglar.

4   Carefully Lee lowered the bucket to the ground below.

Which is the verb in each sentence?

What or who is the subject of each sentence?

D   Now work out some ideas of your own.

Find an interesting or unusual verb in the dictionary. Choose a subject for it. Then make up a short sentence out of the subject and the verb.

One or more members of your group have to act out the sentence.

Carry on until everyone has had a turn.

Don't forget that more than one person or thing at a time can be a subject. For example:

*The **boys** played football in their lunch hour.*

Time past

Verbs are words which have **tenses**.
Tenses are to do with time - the **past, present** and **future**.

A Look at the entry for the word **play¹**.

> **play¹** *verb* (**plays, playing, played**)
> **1** to take part in a game .....

Which form of the verb - **play, plays, playing** or **played** - would you use if you were talking about the past (things that have already happened)?

B What is the past tense of each of the following verbs? (In the dictionary, the past tense is always third in the list of forms.)

walk   jump   pick   climb

What is the rule for turning them into the past tense?

C In what way is the spelling of the past tense of these verbs different?

skip   hop   drag   ram   propel   stir

D How do you spell the past tense of these verbs?

hurry   worry   bully   cry   reply

What is different about them?

E What about the past tense of these verbs that end in **-e** ?

whine   decide   explode   care   provoke

When the past tense of a verb ends in **-d** or **-ed**, you call it a **regular** verb because it follows a rule.

Many verbs are **irregular**.

F   Find the past tense of these:

  shine   **win**   **speak**   **teach**   **catch**   **think**

Are they regular or irregular?

G   Put these verbs into the past tense, and say what you notice about them:

  leap   **creep**   **sleep**   **keep**   **dream**   **feel**   **mean**

H   Which of these verbs are regular and which are irregular?

  stay   **go**   **depart**   **leave**   **split** (meaning 3)

I   What do you notice about the past tense of these verbs?

  know   **blow**   **fly**   **draw**   **throw**

J   These words all sound (and look) alike:

  shake   **wake**   **take**   **make**   **bake**

Do their past tenses sound (and look) alike too?

More about tenses

Sometimes the **past** tense of a verb has its own entry in the dictionary.

> **wrote** past tense of **write.**

A Look up these words:

>   **ate**   **drank**   **grew**   **shrank**

What does the dictionary say about them?

B Look up the verbs:

>   **cooked**   **boiled**   **chopped**   **stirred**

Do they have their own entries. If not, where must you look for them?

C Find out which of these past tense verbs have their own entries:

>   **rose**   **played**   **rang**   **drew**   **forgot**

Discussion

Can you think of a reason why some past tense verbs have their own separate entries and others do not?

Some verbs have an extra **past** tense, called the **past participle.**

> **make** *verb* (makes, making, made)

> **take** *verb* (takes, taking, took, taken)

The past participle is for using with **'has'**, **'had'**, **'was'**, etc.

D Use the right forms of the verbs **make** and **take** to complete these sentences:

1 Sheena **made** a mistake: she _ _ _ _ the wrong train.

2 Sheena has _ _ _ _ a mistake: she has _ _ _ _ _ the wrong train.

E Use the right forms of the verb **give** to complete this sentence:

I have _ _ _ _ _ her the message that you _ _ _ _ me.

Which form is the past participle?

F Use the dictionary to find the past tense and the past participle of each of these verbs:

eat   wake   write   speak   do

What is the ordinary past tense of each of these verbs?

G Find the past tense and the past participle of each of these verbs, and say what you notice about them:

find   keep   buy   sell   lose   spend

All tensed up

The **present** tense is used for what is happening now, or at the time when you are speaking or writing.

> As he **crosses** the finishing line he **throws** his arms triumphantly in the air.

The **future** tense is used for what is going to happen.

> The match **will be** over in just a few minutes, and by the look of it the All-Stars **will win** the championship yet again.

A The following report is written in the **past** tense. Rewrite it in the **present** tense, as though you are talking about things as they happen.

It **was** the last lap of the Italian Grand Prix and Greg, with a huge lead, **was** almost certain of victory. Suddenly, without warning one of his rear tyres **exploded**. The car **went** into a spin, and **crashed** sickeningly into the barriers. The rescue team **ran** in to assist, but thankfully the driver **was** already climbing out unhurt. You **could** see the anger and disappointment on his face as he **pointed** to the shattered machine.

B In which tense is each of the following sentences?

1 Greg **drives** Formula One racing cars.

2 Greg **will** not **drive** again this year.

3 Greg **drove** a brilliant race.

4 He **has driven** to victory six times.

5 He **was driving** cars when he **was** only eleven years old.

6 He**'ll be driving** again next season.

How? When? Where?

Adverbs are words which tell us when or where or how something happens.

A   **yesterday**   **here**   **hurriedly**   **up**

sometimes   **easily**

Which of these six adverbs say *when?*

Which of them say *where* or *where to?*

Which of them say *how?*

B   Adverbs and verbs work together in sentences. Put the six verbs below and the six adverbs from above together. Which works best with which?

won   **dressed**   **arrived**   **try**   **climb**   **wait**

C   Find an adverb which would work well with each of these verbs.

press   **float**   **damage**   **repair**   **penetrate**

For each of your adverbs say whether it says *how*, *when* or *where*.

D   Adverbs are often made by adding **-ly** to other words.

Which words do these adverbs come from? Be careful with ones that end in **-ily**.

slowly
warily
hungrily
particularly
finally

Drama

Find the adverbs in the following sentences and look them up in your copy of *The Oxford Primary School Dictionary*:

> They did the job sloppily and half-heartedly. The manager paid them reluctantly and told them not to come back again.

Discuss how the people behaved in these two sentences. A group of you can work out a short play showing how they acted.

Here is another short play:

> In the centre of the stage there is a table. On it is an envelope. Nicky enters, goes **immediately** to the table and picks up the envelope **inquisitively.**

Act the scene through, with one of the group as Nicky and another giving directions.

Try changing one or both of the adverbs (**immediately** and **inquisitively**) and then performing the scene again. You could try some of the following adverbs, using the dictionary to help you.

indignantly   expectantly   directly   indifferently
defiantly   hesitantly   impulsively   discreetly

Discussion

How much did the adverbs make a difference to your acting?

Compound words

A **compound word** is a word made from two shorter words. For example:

nightfall = night + fall

A Here is a selection of short words. How many **compound words** can you make from them? (You can use *The Oxford Primary School Dictionary* to help you.)

> **green   house   boat   flood   floor   light**
>
> **out   ever   hold   work   board   side**
>
> **post   strong   man**

You can use any word more than once.

B How many compound words can you think of that begin with **over-**?

When you have listed as many as you can, look in the dictionary to see how many there are there.

Can you think of some compound words that end with **-over**?

C Put the following pairs of words together and look up the resulting words in *The Oxford Primary School Dictionary*. What do you notice about the spelling of all of them?

> **look + alike**   **leap + frog**
>
> **hard + boiled**   **full + time**
>
> **hide + and + seek**   **no + man's + land**

The game of Word Dominoes

You can use compound words to make *Word Dominoes.* Here is a game that has been started.

Can you make any new dominoes to continue the game? You can go in any direction; and you can use the dictionary to help you find new words.

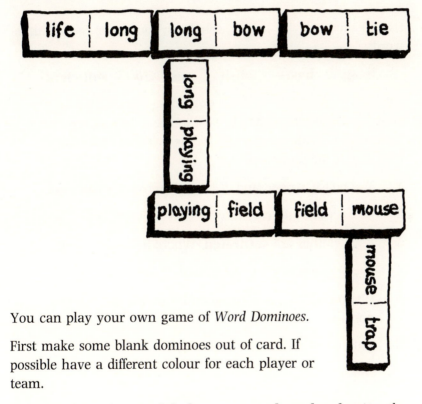

You can play your own game of *Word Dominoes.*

First make some blank dominoes out of card. If possible have a different colour for each player or team.

The first player (or team) finds a compound word and writes the two parts of it on one of the dominoes. The others, in turn, try to build out from the first domino, as in the example above.

If you cannot think of a word, you miss a turn. When nobody can think of any more words, the game ends, and the player or team with the most dominoes on the table wins.

All the same

The two tubes contain the same stuff. The two words **glue** and **adhesive** mean the same.
Words that mean the same are called **synonyms**.

A   Use the dictionary to help you find a synonym for each of these words:

       heap   **haste**   **dish**   **cast** *verb*   **sufficient**

B   Look up the words printed in bold in the following sentences. Try to replace them with other single words, without changing the meaning of the sentences:

1   The police arrived and at once the crowds **dispersed.**

2   Be **exceedingly** careful with that package.

3   Your clothes are **saturated**. Where have you been?

4   She is **generally** late for school.

5   His **initial** plan was to **ascend** the mountain on the north side.

6   Only a few snakes are **venomous**.

Discussion

Can you think why there are sometimes two or more words with the same meaning?

Is it *useful* to have two or more words that mean the same? If so, why?

The game of Synonyms

Here are 15 pairs of words which mean the same as each other - only they are all mixed up.

**similar   brag   rich   amicable   forbidden
exact   bucket   absurd   costly   boast
ridiculous   perfect   fracture   inscribed
barrel   suitable   rubbish   written   expensive
pail   cask   banned   precise   affluent
friendly   break   comparable   ideal
garbage   appropriate**

Write each word on a card and place all the cards face down on a table.

Take turns to turn over two cards so that everyone can see them. If they mean the same thing, keep them and have another go straight away. If they do not mean the same thing, turn them face down again and your turn ends.

The player who ends up with the most pairs, wins.

You can use *The Oxford Primary School Dictionary* to look up the words before and during this game.

Opposites

These pairs of words mean the **opposite** of each other.

high, low   wet, dry   difficult, easy

A   Think of an opposite for each of these words:

top   long   loud   rapid   front

B   Look these up in the dictionary and then think of a word that is the opposite of each one:

fragrant   fruitless   genuine   remote

casual   occasional

C   A lot of words can be made to mean the opposite by adding one of these to the beginning:

un- in- im- il- ir- anti-

They are called **prefixes**.

Choose the correct prefix for each of these words to turn them into their opposites. Try each in turn until you find a dictionary entry for each opposite.

possible   legal   necessary   secure

responsible   clockwise

D   Make these sentences mean the opposite by changing one or more words in each of them.

The accident was unavoidable.
The children behaved in a very immature way.
Colin's writing is illegible.
The drummer beat a loud and irregular rhythm.
He was an unkind and intolerant man.

The game of Opposites

Look at the game called *Synonyms* on page 39.

You can play a similar game, following the same rules, using pairs of words that are opposites.

Here are a few pairs of opposites mixed up. You can add a few others yourselves, with the help of the dictionary.

up   massive   fortunate   cruel   careful
gradually   internal   negative   useful
minute   obey   useless   suddenly   disobey
positive   external   lowered   certain
unlucky   careless   down   kind
raised   doubtful

Shopping

A Look up the words for these shops and then make a short list of some of the things you could buy in each one:

newsagent **delicatessen** **boutique** **greengrocer**

B Which of the following would you find in a **hardware** shop?

lentils **brackets** **washers** **swedes**

C   Supermarkets have signs above the shelves to help you find the
things you want.

Look at the picture opposite. Copy it and write the names of these
goods on the shelves where they belong:

    courgettes   **oatmeal**   **muesli**   **yoghurt**

    swedes   **yams**   **cream**   **spinach**   **Cheddar**

D   Look at the table below.

Across the top are shops. Down the side are the first letters of goods
you can buy in these shops. For example:

    plug begins with **p** and a **plug** is **electrical**

	electrical shop	clothes shop	food shop
p	plug		
r			
b			
t			
w			

To complete the table you have to put one correct *noun* in each box.
See how many you can find, using the dictionary to help you.

Try making a similar table with different shops and different letters.
You can make your own game out of completing the table. Decide
on rules before you begin. (For example, you could give an extra
point for any word no one else in your group has thought of.)

Crossword

Clues

The first letter of each answer is given to you.

Across

1   *verb* to keep someone or something safe (P)

7   *adjective* ready to be harvested or eaten (R)

8   *noun* a mixture of smoke and fog (S)

9   *noun* what you can see from one place (V)

10   *noun* a circle (R)

12   *noun* a person who does gymnastics (G)

Down

2   *noun* a small, soft, red fruit (R)

3   *verb* to pull something along behind you (T)

4   *noun* the best people in sports, competitions, etc. (C)

5   *noun* a small house on wheels (C)

6   *adjective* having promised to marry someone (E)

11   *verb* past tense of **win** (W)

Here are some more clues. See if you can work them out:

A   A car can [3 across] a [5 down].

B   People often wear a [10 across] when they are [6 down].

C   You should not eat a [2 down] until it is [7 across]

D   [8 across] can spoil the [9 down]

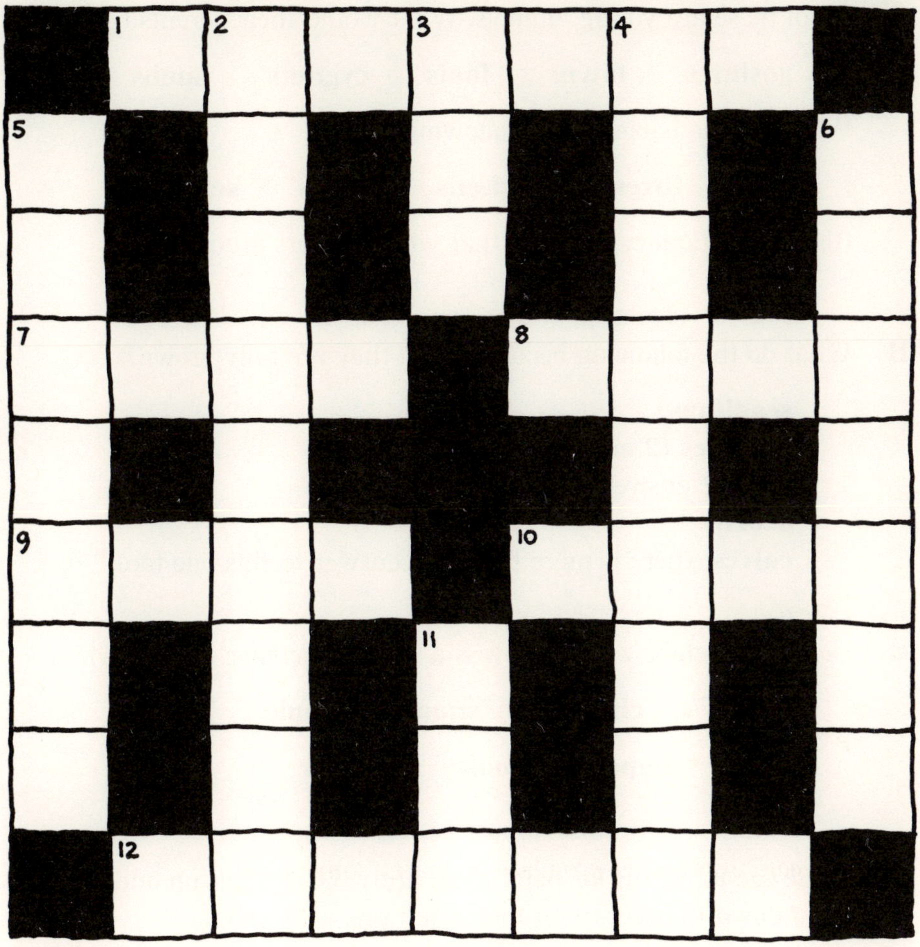

Little and large

A All of these are young animals. What would their parents be?

    goslings   **fawns**   **foals**   **cygnets**   **lambs**

What are the babies of the following called?

    cats   **foxes**   **chickens**   **ducks**   **seals**

(Use the dictionary to check that your answers are right.)

B What do the following become when they are fully grown?

    seedlings
    tadpoles (2 answers possible)
    kids (2 answers possible)
    acorns
    calves (there is more than one answer to this one too)

C Each of the eight words below is a small *something*: a small what?

    dinghy   **chuckle**   **snack**   **ripple**

    nap   **chapel**   **brook**   **splinter**

D These are all words for parts of an army. Look them up and write them down in order, with the largest one at the top.

    company   **brigade**   **platoon**   **battalion**   **division**

E What are these?

    a **piglet**   a **booklet**   a **minibus**

F Put these *adjectives* into order, starting with the one meaning largest:

> **minute**   **sizeable**   **microscopic**   **immense**
>
> **infinite**   **small**

G There are two sets of five words below, all mixed up. Can you make them into two lists, with the strongest at the top and the weakest at the bottom?

> **loud**   **dim**   **soft**   **brilliant**
>
> **thunderous**   **inaudible**   **bright**
>
> **deafening**   **dazzling**   **invisible**

H Sometimes people make up their own words for small things.

Just for fun, try making up a word for each of these. Put the plurals in the brackets.

> .... *noun* (........)
> a small street with houses on both sides,
> but no room for cars to park.

> .... *noun* (........)
> a very short lesson on a Friday afternoon.

> .... *noun* (........)
> a small piece of chocolate broken off a big
> bar, by someone who is not very generous.

Whose suggestions do you think are the best? Whose are funniest?

Shape and space

A Copy the shapes and give them their correct names.

cone   **cylinder**   **cuboid**   **semicircle**

parallelogram   **pentagon**

prism

B   Draw a **set-square** and say what it is used for.

C   What is the **radius** of a circle?

You can answer in words, or by drawing.

D   List three things which have the shape of a **sphere**.

E   Which is the larger area: a **hectare** or an **acre**?

F   Which of these two shapes can form a **tesselation** and which cannot?

hexagon   octagon

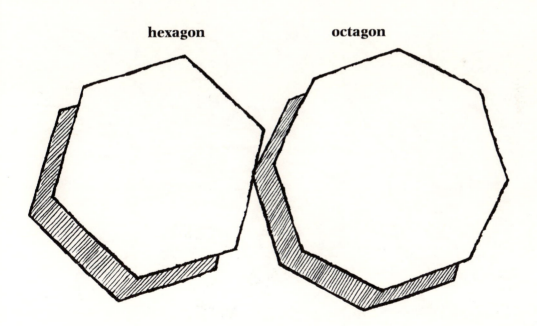

Going places

A   Copy or trace the map of *Spagland* on the facing page.

Here are the names - and descriptions - of some of the places in *Spagland*. Put the names on the map where you think they should go. (Looking up the words in bold type might help you.)

> *Spag Heights* - a mountain **range.**
>
> *The Rollers* - **downs** (see **down³**).
>
> *The Snake* - an **isthmus**.
>
> *Bad point* - a narrow **spit.**
>
> *The Shark's Teeth* - a dangerous **reef.**
>
> *The Sisters* - the islands in the **gulf.**
>
> *Square Head* - the large **peninsula.**
>
> *The River Slug* - the river that **meanders** across the **plain.**
>
> *Snag Brook* - the **tributary** of the *Slug.*
>
> *Big Mouth* - the Slug **estuary.**
>
> *The Spoon* - an **inlet.**
>
> *Whitesands* - a small **cove.**

B   Write a short tourist guide to *Spagland*, mentioning some of the places you have put on the map.

All in the past

Look at the time line on the opposite page.

It starts with early times and finishes with the year **2000**.

A   Make a copy of the time line and the boxes. Then look up these abbreviations in *The Oxford Primary School Dictionary:*

   AD   BC

Put them in the correct *square* boxes on your time line diagram.

Write the names **Julius Caesar** and **Christopher Columbus** and join them with arrows to the time line.

B   Use the dictionary to put each of these words in the right *rectangular* boxes:

   Tudors   Victorians   Vikings

C   Look up the words **armada** and **civil**. Use them to add three important events to the time line.

D   Write these words alongside the time line *roughly* where they belong:

   cohort   ballista   galley   pyramid

   galleon   legion   centurian

   knight   keep   consul

(One has been done as an example.) Looking up the word **ancient** may help.

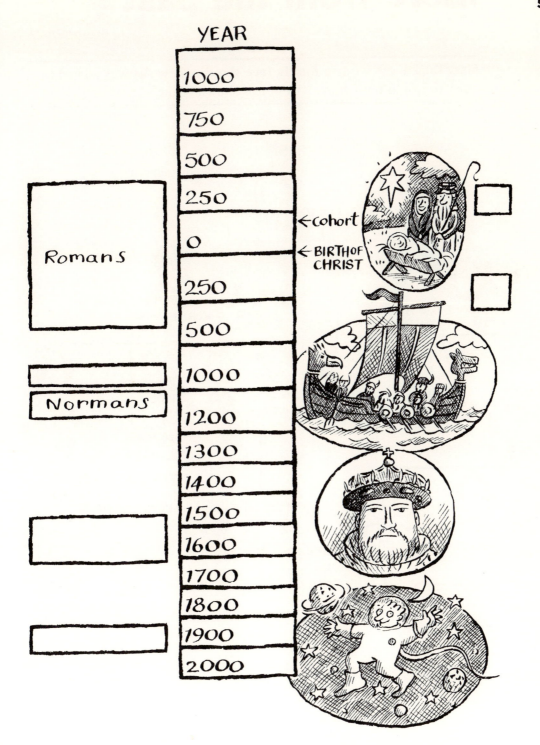

YEAR

1000
750
500
250
0
250
500
1000
1200
1300
1400
1500
1600
1700
1800
1900
2000

← cohort

← BIRTH OF CHRIST

Romans

Normans

More from the past

Mary Duckworth wrote a **family tree** showing how she was related to other people in her family. Part of it is shown below.

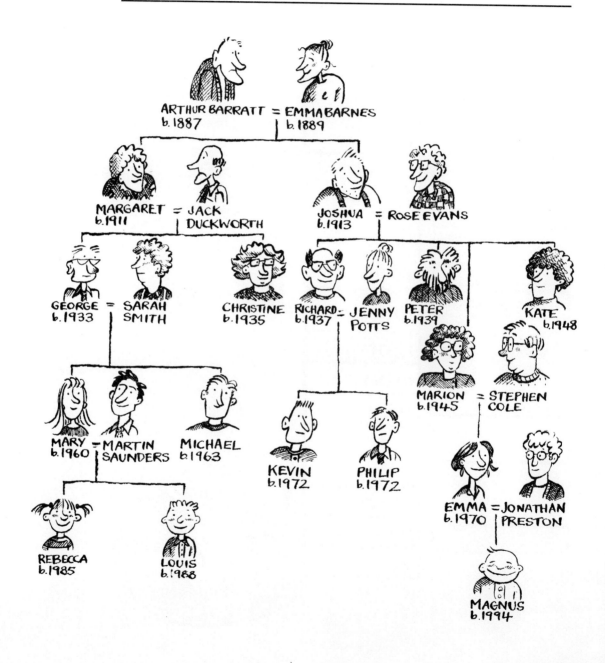

The equals sign means that the two people joined by it married one another. Emma Barratt's name was Emma Barnes before she married Arthur. Margaret and Joshua were Arthur and Emma's children. The dates next to people's names tell you when they were born.

A 1 How many **generations** are shown on the family tree?

2 How many **descendants** has Arthur Barratt got?

3 Name two of Mary Duckworth's **ancestors**.

4 Give the names of Margaret Barratt's **nephews** and **nieces**.

5 Who was Jenny Potts's **father-in-law**?

6 The letters *dd.* are short for **deceased**. What does this mean?

B Try writing part of your **family tree** showing some of your **relatives**.

Science quiz

A Try to answer the questions. Use your dictionary to see how many you got right.

1 What would you measure in **decibels**?
A: heat   B: height   C: sound   D: weight

2 An **asteroid** is a small:
A: planet   B: flower   C: fish   D: river

3 A **dynamo** produces:
A: food   B: electricity   C: steam   D: noise

4 Which of these is a **citrus** fruit?
A: raspberry   B: melon   C: apple   D: grapefruit

5 A **vertebrate** is an animal with:
A: a brain   B: a backbone   C: cold blood   D: warm blood

6 Which of these is a **predator** of the frog?
A: the toad   B: the heron   C: the tadpole
D: the water lily

7 Which of the following is closest in meaning to **velocity**?
A: weight   B: speed   C: energy   D: distance

8 An **amphibian** lives:
A: on land   B: in water   C: on land and in water
D: in trees

9 Which of the following is part of the **digestive system**?
A: lungs   B: stomach   C: heart   D: nerves

10 **Respiration** is:
A: sweating   B: exercising   C: breathing   D: resting

```
M  T  H  Y  A  D  C  H  R  D  G  T
O  M  I  C  R  O  S  C  O  P  E  B
S  A  B  A  T  T  E  R  Y  A  Q  O
S  M  B  L  C  X  F  O  E  N  U  S
K  M  O  L  A  V  A  C  O  T  A  T
L  A  I  O  L  Q  P  O  W  E  T  A
T  L  J  Y  C  R  G  D  V  N  O  A
U  K  Y  S  I  H  F  I  E  N  R  W
A  M  E  J  U  I  M  L  N  A  D  N
L  R  E  Z  M  A  U  E  N  E  V  C
```

B Can you find the words for these things hidden among the letters in the square?

1   Something which stores electricity.

2   The feelers on the head of an insect.

3   A mixture of metals.

4   The line around the middle of the earth.

5   An animal that feeds its young on milk.

6   A mineral which strengthens teeth and bones.

7   A large reptile.

8   An instrument which magnifies objects.

9   A non-flowering plant.

10   Molten rock that flows from a volcano.

Collectors' items

These words belong to a set or collection:

{ igloo   shack   mansion   flat }

A Can you think of any other words which belong to the same set?

Can you think of a word for all the things in the set?

B Here is another collection:

{ aluminium   copper   zinc   lead }

Look them up in the dictionary and say what they all are.

C Collect three more words to go with these:

{ amber   indigo   crimson }

and give a name to the set.

D Look up these words, and say what they all are:

{ pout   scowl   grimace }

Can you add three more words which belong in the set?

E In the list below there are two sets of words mixed up:

ballet   morris   flamingo   flamenco

grouse   plover   reel   wagtail

Look them up and sort them out into two separate sets.

F   There is an odd word out in the following collection. Which do you think it is and why?

        oyster   lobster   squid   limpet   cockle   whelk

G   Who might do all of the following things as part of his or her job?

        cultivate   sow   harvest   reap

What else might the same person do?

H   One of these should not be in the collection. It is the odd one out.

        sovereign   monarch   president   citizen   ruler

Which do you think it is, and why?

I   Look up the word **lethal** in the dictionary.

Make a collection of five things which are, or can be, **lethal**.

Words and music

oboe   **clarinet**   **bassoon**

A These are all **wind instruments**. What else can you find out about them from the dictionary?

B How many musical words can you find that begin with the letters **pi-?**

C A detective discovered that a **suspect** in a case had been to a concert on the night of the crime; but, it turned out, he had missed the **overture.** Do you think the suspect had:

1 arrived late for the concert?

2 slipped out in the middle?

3 left before the end?

D In which order would you put the following words, and why?

alto   baritone   bass   soprano   tenor

E   What is similar about these kinds of music:

      rock   **reggae**   **jazz**

Choose one of them and write a sentence or two about it, using the dictionary, and, if you like, other reference books to help you.

F   If someone felt like singing the **blues**, what sort of mood do you think he or she would be in?

G   Give some examples of **percussion** instruments. How many of these have you played?

H   What is the name of the note an **octave** above the note 'C' ?

I   How many musicians are there in a **quartet**?

J   What have the following wind instruments got in common?

      trumpet   **trombone**   **French horn**   **tuba**

Which two of them are most alike?

Draw pictures of three of them.

People and places

For some of these questions, try looking in the back of your dictionary - in the part called *Appendices*.

You will also find an **atlas** useful for some of the tasks.

A   What do we call the people of the countries named on the map?

B   Make a copy of the map and mark in the names of the countries where these people live:

French   **Hungarians**   **Poles**

Turks   **Austrians**   **Spaniards**

WEAR A GREEN KIRTLE

Betrothed in infancy, Catherine Sackville, now sixteen, journeys to Norfolk to meet her husband-to-be for the first time. Thomas, Viscount Bindon, cold and aloof, seems no more eager for the match than she; and Catherine, discovering he has already sired a bastard, resentful and forlorn, longs to return home.

Henry of Surrey, Thomas's brother, incurs the King's displeasure and is charged with treason, and Thomas too is implicated and arrested. Catherine must now return to her family – as she had wished. But somehow ... Only then, at the moment of farewell, does she recognize her true feelings.

Wear a Green Kirtle is Philippa Wiat's sixth novel about the flamboyant House of Howard.

PHILIPPA WIAT

Wear a Green Kirtle

ROBERT HALE · LONDON

© Philippa Wiat 1987
First published in Great Britain 1987

ISBN 0 7090 3003 7

Robert Hale Limited
Clerkenwell House
Clerkenwell Green
London EC1R 0HT

Photoset in North Wales by
Derek Doyle & Associates, Mold, Clwyd.
Printed in Great Britain by
St Edmundsbury Press Ltd, Bury St Edmunds, Suffolk
Bound by WBC Bookbinders Limited.

The Prologue

"So there you are!" growled the boy's stepfather from the seat in the inglenook. "Decided to come home at last, have you?"

The boy nodded and carefully deposited an armful of firewood in front of the hearth, before turning to close the door that gave entrance to the farmhouse kitchen.

"Cat got your tongue, boy?" the man asked angrily. "Come here and tell me why you're late."

"Leave him alone, Jake," pleaded his wife. "'Tis not his fault he's late – I sent him to gather firewood."

The man ignored her. "Your brothers and sisters have been in bed long since. So why are you still around, cluttering up the place as usual? Tell me and be quick about it, or 'twill be the worse for you."

"I am older than they are," said the boy, with a touch of pride. "I'm seven."

"So you're seven, are you?" sneered the man. "Very interesting. If I recall correctly, I married your ma only six years ago. So what does that make you?"

The boy gazed silently back at him. The expression in his dark eyes was unfathomable, and already his youthful figure gave hint of a nobility that was a provocation to the man.

"I asked you two questions, boy, and still I be waiting for the answers. First, I want to know why you're late home so that your ma's been crying her eyes out with worry, instead of –" The man glanced pointedly at his wife. "– instead of giving her mind to more important matters."

"I wasn't crying because he was late, as well you know," put in his wife. "I knew where he was – 'twas I sent him on the errand, as I told you. You're always picking on him, Jake, blaming him for all that's wrong around here. You know well enough why I was weeping."

"Hold your peace, woman!" ordered the man threateningly, before turning again to the boy. "Since you refuse to answer the first question – a fact I'm noting very carefully – you'd best make haste and answer the second before I lose patience. What does it mean, me marrying your ma after you were born and she still unwed?"

"You've no right to speak so to him," protested the woman. "He's naught but a child."

"No right? Who round here has a better right? Tell me that. This is my farm, you are my wife, and he is my stepson – who has a better right to question him and chastise him when he's wilful and disobedient? He's a bastard – he knows it and I know it. What are you, boy?"

"I am your stepson," said the boy quietly.

"You dare to contradict your betters?"

"I am your stepson," persisted the boy. "You told mama that just now."

"Peter's bones!" thundered the farmer, turning to his wife. "Did you hear that? The lad's taunting me. He's defying me. Did you ever hear the like?"

"Leave him alone, Jake," pleaded his wife. "You're for ever picking on him, specially when the drink's in you. Life's scarcely worth living when you're like this."

"Sorry you married me, are you? Is that what you're saying?"

"Nay, of course not. I love you, my husband – haven't I proved it by giving you five children since we were wed? You knew about James when you married me."

"James!" mimicked the farmer. "James! What a mincing popinjay's name that is, to be sure! What was wrong with a sensible name like Josh or Will or Harry?"

"His Lordship wanted him called James," explained his wife evasively.

"And His Lordship's wants have to be satisfied, as we know," sneered the farmer. "We've living proof of it, haven't we?"

"'Twas because of James and the dowry that came with me that you were able to buy the farm. His Lordship's settlement was generous in the extreme."

"His Lordship's settlement! Pah! His Lordship's settlement was with your father, not with me," retorted the farmer. "I've no doubt your father did well out of the deal – feathered his own nest from the sale of his daughter's maidenhead!"

"May God forgive you for speaking so in front of the boy!" exclaimed his wife. "Father is innkeeper of *The White Lion* right enough – and *he* doesn't spend his days drinking himself daft! Anyway, that's all in the past. You knew what you were about when you married me and it suited you well enough then."

"I was fond of you – that's why I married you," said the farmer angrily. "But always the boy's been there, taunting me by his presence, reminding me that someone else had you before me."

"I loved you, Jake, and still do."

"It didn't seem so a while back, before the boy came in. For weeks you've kept me at arm's length. You pushed me away just then as if you remembered your lover and couldn't bear me to touch you!"

"Till this year, I've given you a child every twelve-month since we wed," the woman said quietly. "I don't want to fall again, as you know. With you ofttimes the worse for drink, the farm's not paying its way, and we don't want another mouth to feed yet awhile."

"We'll talk about that later," said the farmer. "You belong to me now, Drusilla my girl – I've a right to obedience in all things and don't you forget it! 'Tis him on your mind – your fine lover – that makes you refuse me."

"You believe that – after all these years?" She tried to sound scornful but even to herself it seemed unconvincing.

"You'll not pull the wool over my eyes, lass," declared the farmer. "You hanker after him still – but I'll beat it out of you yet!"

"Take care, Jake, that in beating it out of me, as you say, you don't beat out my regard for you at the same time. I'm fond of you – how many more times must I tell you that? What

happened with James's father was a long time ago. Why can't
you forget it? Think you I want to be reminded of my shame?
Always you must be taunting me, tormenting yourself and the
boy – sometimes I think you want to make me hate you!"

"'Twould be all right if he wasn't here," grumbled the man,
nodding in the direction of the boy. "'Tis him as won't let me
forget."

"In a year or so His Lordship will arrange for him to go
away to be educated." Her voice trembled. "Then you won't
be troubled with him any longer."

"Your eyes fill with tears at the very thought of parting with
your by-blow," jeered the farmer, his jealousy feeding his
anger. He turned to the boy. "Why are you standing there
gawking? Enjoy seeing your ma taunt your stepfather, do
you?"

"Nay, stepfather. And I like not to see mama weeping!"

"Enjoy being a bastard, do you?"

The boy made no reply, but merely gazed gravely at his
stepfather. Already he had learned the wisdom of silence.

"Answer me," growled the farmer.

"How can he answer such a question?" put in his wife.
"You are cruel to …"

"How can he answer, you ask?" interposed the farmer.
"With his lips and tongue, of course – being a bastard makes
no difference to that. He's defying me, and I'll have no lecher's
by-blow make mock of me. Down on your knees, boy."

With a quiet dignity that disguised his fear, the boy knelt
down in front of his stepfather.

"You're not fit to lick a decent man's boots, bastard," the
farmer told him. "But fair's fair. Because you're my stepson
and I was paid to wed your ma and give you a roof over your
head, I'll let you do just that. You may lick my boots."

The woman gasped, and the boy looked down at the man's
mud-caked boots.

Then, looking the farmer straight in the eye, he shook his
head.

"I'll not do it, stepfather," he said firmly. "And you'll not
make me."

"Ho-ho! What have we here? A bastard who defies his betters. So you believe I'll not make you – we'll have to see about that!"

Without removing his gaze from the boy, the farmer unbuckled his thick leather belt and reached out for him.

"You'll do it, bastard, you'll do it – if I have to whip you raw first," he said through clenched teeth. "I'll ..."

As in sudden fear the boy struggled to free himself from his stepfather's powerful grasp, his mother stepped forward.

Slender and frail in contrast to her powerfully built husband, the unexpectedness of her attack took him momentarily off guard.

Thrusting her hands against his chest, she loosened his grip on her son and pulled him away.

"Run, James," she said urgently. "Make for the woods like you did last time – and come not back till you see a candle burning in the attic window and know that all's well."

With a furious oath, the farmer reached out to grab the boy, but his wife stood between them.

"Run, James. Away with you!" she cried, watching anxiously till he had reached the door and lifted the latch. "Stay your hand till he's gone, my husband. Then you can vent your wrath on me. Your quarrel's not with him, is it? It never was ..."

Slamming the door behind him, his heart thumping, the boy ran towards the tall trees on the further side of the cornfield. Dusk was approaching but darkness held no terrors for him. Out there he was free as the wind; free as the screech owls and the bats. Out there he was no longer a bastard.

But even as he made his escape, a sound reached him from the farmhouse that stopped him in his tracks.

He turned and ran light-footed back to the house, drawn by the scream – his mother's scream.

He halted at the door and listened. Trembling, he heard the leather belt descend again and again on naked flesh. He heard his mother's cries; and his stepfather's voice, thick with drink and lust and fury, raised in blind accusation.

Frightened and sick at heart, he hesitated, not sure whether to go to his mother's assistance.

Such scenes of violence were not new to him. His stepfather's anger was quickly roused and his hand frequently raised against him or his mother – though rarely against his own children. He had ofttimes lain awake in the attic chamber he shared with his half-brothers, listening fearfully and unwillingly to the sounds of his stepfather's voice and hand raised in anger against his mother.

Run away, his mother had said. One day I shall run away for good, he thought to himself. I shall go and look for my father, my real father, and ask him to help mama and me.

Several times already I have seen my father – mama leaves me at *The White Lion,* my grandfather's inn in the village, and grandfather takes me to an upstairs chamber where my father, who everyone addresses as His Lordship, awaits me. His Lordship is kind but says little – he seems at a loss what to say to me – so I too say little, though always I long to ask him who he is. After a while, he gives me a gold piece and tells me to be a good boy, to love mama and go with God. Then he summons grandfather and bids me farewell.

When I get home, mama tells me to give the gold piece to stepfather, and stepfather frowns and seems not at all pleased with it – I know not why. I try to be a good boy like His Lordship told me, and of course I do love mama – always. But I know not how to go with God: perchance one day, when I leave home so that mama can be happy without me there to make stepfather angry, God will be waiting for me and I shall go with him to find my father …

His reverie ceased abruptly as he heard his stepfather throw down the leather belt. Tears streamed unheeded down his cheeks and, trying to still his sobs lest he be overheard, he crept along to a small window and peered into the farm kitchen.

He stared in dismay. His stepfather was holding his mother face-down across his knees while she, her petticoats thrown back, lay quiet and unresisting.

She was weeping softly, as if she had long since recognized the futility of her pleas. He could see the wheals that criss-crossed her pale skin, reddening it from thighs to buttocks.

Even as he watched in mingled horror and fascination, he saw his stepfather release her and get to his feet.

"That'll help you forget your fine lover!" he said thickly, towering over her.

"On the contrary," she said with sudden spirit. "Your brutality but serves to remind me of his gentleness!"

"You bitch!" he said. "Will you never cease from taunting me? Have I to teach you further?"

"Oh, the lesson was well learned," she said bitterly. "My bruised flesh will keep me from sleep and I shall have all night to think upon your cruelty!"

"Forgive me," he said then. "I meant not to lay it on so hard. I was goaded by jealousy."

"Jealousy or lust?"

"I'm jealous all right – God knows I'm jealous! It's the boy. Always he comes between us. Always he reminds me of his begetting, and how it was with you and his father."

"'Twas all so long ago," she said tremulously. "So very long ago."

"Take me not for a fool, woman!" he said roughly. "Think you I notice not how, when your lover's name is mentioned, a tenderness comes over your face that's never there for me?"

"You imagine it," she told him. "You imagine it and then you blame the child. I love not His Lordship. Never did I love him. 'Tis you I love – how many more times must I tell you?"

"Prove it then," he said gruffly. "Last time, you pushed me away."

"I want not another child."

"You'll have what you're given and like it," he said, his temper rising again.

With that, he took a knife from the table and, ignoring her startled protests, cut the laces of her gown. Released from the confining bodice, her breasts spilled out, swaying provocatively.

Guessing his intention then, she tried to draw away – but too late. He drew her down on to the rush-strewn floor and leaned over her, fondling her breasts and watching her expression curiously.

"Nay –" she wept, "– not now. Leave me be, I beg you …"

"Leave you be? Not likely," he said savagely. "You are mine, by God – not his! You are mine to do with as I will!"

"Not another child, Jake," she pleaded. "'Twill be my death if I have another so soon. The midwife warned me the last time – little Henry nearly cost me my life …"

"Fiddle-faddle! Women's nonsense. What's a woman for but childbearing – tell me that? A fine body you have, wife – ripe for giving a man pleasure and bearing his children."

Roused by jealousy and his own brutality, his very words served to increase his lust.

"Nay, nay … !" she cried hysterically, trying in vain to release herself. "For pity's sake – you're hurting me. My belly … "

She screamed, and the watching boy, frightened by a scene he had no means of understanding, pressed a fist to his mouth to stifle his sobs.

He turned away, and ran from the house as fast as his legs could carry him, not pausing until he had reached the shelter of the tall trees.

Then he flung himself down on the mossy turf and wept as if his heart were broken.

"Soon I shall – run – away – for – good," he sobbed. "Then stepfather will stop being angry with mama. I shall run away to my real father – him they call His Lordship. He will love me – I know he will!"

One

"You sent for me, my lord," Catherine said, entering the spacious, oak-panelled chamber that was her father's library. "You wish to speak with me on a matter of importance, I am told."

Henry Sackville, Earl of Dorset, nodded. "I do indeed, daughter. Pray be seated," he said.

Catherine did as she was bid and, from the high-backed velvet-cushioned chair, watched her father anxiously. His stern visage and air of formality suggested that this was no ordinary summons. This then, as she had feared, was THE SUMMONS – the one she had dreaded for many weeks past.

"Doubtless you have guessed what I am about to say, daughter," Lord Dorset said then. "Today being the twenty-fourth of September and your sixteenth birthday, methinks it will come as no surprise to you."

"This is surely the most exciting of birthdays, papa," declared Catherine, in a desperate attempt to divert her father from what he was about to say. "You yourself have given me a beautiful pearl necklace, my sisters have given me handkerchiefs embroidered by their own hands, and cook has baked a cake especially to …"

Lord Dorset cut short Catherine's chatter.

"Yesterday a messenger arrived from the Duke of Norfolk," he told her. "He brought a letter from His Grace that concerns your future."

"Indeed, papa?" asked Catherine, her smile vanishing.

"His Grace suggests that two weeks hence you set forth for Kenninghall, his Norfolk palace, there to make the acquaintance of your husband-to-be," Lord Dorset said

13

quietly. "The messenger left here this morning, carrying my letter to the Duke approving his suggestion."

"But, papa, the weather is inclement for journeying – it is several days' ride to Kenninghall," protested Catherine, clutching at straws.

"It is September, my daughter – not mid-winter," pointed out Lord Dorset. "You are strong, healthy and an expert horsewoman, and can well withstand the rigours of such a journey. On my faith, I have never before known you give heed to the weather!"

"You have never before asked me to undertake such a journey, papa – never in all my life have I been beyond the boundaries of Dorset. Could not I wait till the spring?" pleaded Catherine. "I have no wish to miss Edward's wedding, and Cecily and Meg … "

"Spare me such prevarications, daughter," smiled Lord Dorset. "Tell me instead your true reason for wishing to postpone your departure."

Catherine's eyes filled with tears. "Alas, papa, how can I go! Sackville Hall has been my home all my life. I know naught of the world beyond. How can I leave you, and my brothers and sisters? My sisters are children as yet – they depend on me greatly since mama died."

For a long moment Lord Dorset watched her consideringly. In truth, he was sorrowful at the thought of losing her and hoped he had made the right decision. From every aspect it was an excellent match, for she was to become the bride of the second son of the richest and most powerful noble in England. His voice was firm when he spoke, and gave no hint of his feelings.

"As my lady is dead, God rest her soul, it is incumbent upon myself to remind you that, were she here now, she would urge you to your duty. She came here to Sackville in much the same way as you will be going to Kenninghall. There is no need for me to tell you, daughter, of the happiness we shared, or of my continuing sense of loss since her death. I pray that you and your lord will come to know happiness such as was ours."

"But Viscount Bindon is a stranger, papa," persisted

Catherine. "I have not once seen him."

"Your mother had not seen me ere she came here to Sackville as a sixteen year old bride," came the answer. "His Lordship is in his twenty-seventh year and is the second son of the third Duke of Norfolk. He has waited a long time for his bride – you were betrothed by proxy when you were three years old and he was fourteen. Now, with the advent of your sixteenth birthday, we can delay the marriage no longer. After the Nuptial Mass, His Lordship will make you truly his bride."

"We are to be married as soon as I reach Kenninghall?" asked Catherine uneasily.

"You are going to Kenninghall in October and, in accordance with my agreement with the Duke, will be married at Westminster Abbey three months later – on 20th January," explained Lord Dorset. "Thus, my daughter, will you be given the opportunity of first getting to know His Lordship and his family, as well as the vast estates in Norfolk and Suffolk over which the Duke presides. That will pave the way for your becoming Viscount Bindon's bride."

"But, papa, dearest papa ..."

"No more buts, my daughter," interposed Lord Dorset, closing his heart to her pleading. "I have been patient with you because I understand your reluctance to leave your home and family. But none of us may choose our path in life – and certainly not a young maiden of noble lineage."

"How can I, papa?"

"How can you what?"

"How can I bid farewell to my home and family, perchance for ever, and go to live among strangers? And, papa, how could I ... ?" Catherine's voice floundered into silence and she demurely lowered her gaze.

Lord Dorset watched her for a few moments, guessing what was troubling her. Loving her for her likeness to the beloved wife he had lost, he was torn between love and expediency.

She reminds me so vividly of my first meeting with her mother, he thought. *She has the same light blonde hair and green eyes, the same air of gentleness and innocence that belies her shapely figure and the warmth of her voice.*

"Speak that which is in your mind, daughter," he said.

"Papa, how could I – how could I bed with a stranger?"

"By your bridal day, His Lordship will be no longer a stranger."

"All the same, papa ..."

"There is no more to be said, Catherine." Lord Dorset stood up, thus making it plain that the conversation was at an end. "Make up your mind here and now that you will be setting forth for Kenninghall in fourteen days' time. Your bridal gown and trousseau have been ready these twelve months past, and I shall arrange for men-at-arms and your personal maid to escort you on the journey."

"Then Brigid is going with me?" asked Catherine, on a note of cheer.

"Only on the journey. She will return with the men-at-arms on the day following your arrival."

"Papa, I beg you to reconsider," pleaded Catherine tearfully. "Brigid was my nurse and ever since mama died has been like a second mother to Cecily, Margaret, Ann and me – pray grant me this one request!"

"Methought of having Brigid remain with you, but the Duke considers it advisable that you make a clean break with Sackville," explained Lord Dorset. "I was swayed also by the realization that your sisters, being of tender years, have need of Brigid's motherliness – and she herself will be getting married some day."

"But Brigid is quite old, papa – she is in her thirty-second year!"

"She and Silas, the woodcutter, have been walking out together these five years past."

"I know, papa. She always speaks of him as 'my intended' but I doubt she will marry him. She means to remain with us for always – we are like her own children!"

"I have spoken to her on the subject, my daughter, and it seems that, knowing how much you and your sisters needed her, she told Silas she would stay on till you had attained your sixteenth birthday," explained Lord Dorset. "Now, she and Silas will marry and live in a cottage on the estate. Thus will she be able, as she put it, to keep a close eye on your sisters. So you see, Catherine, the matter has been decided for us. Like you, my dear, Brigid has another path to follow."

"You say, papa, that the Duke considers it advisable that I make a clean break with Sackville. Does he then wish me never to see my family again?"

"Nay, it is merely that he sees a clean break as the easiest way of adapting to a new life. Once you are wed, you and your husband will ofttimes visit us here at Sackville, I doubt not."

"I hope it will be as you say, papa," Catherine said, as if she had doubt of it. "The Duke is surely cruel and heartless – already I hate him and doubtless I shall hate his son also!"

"Some would share your sentiments regarding the Duke," admitted Lord Dorset. "I myself have found him to be a gentleman of courage and charm – of his son I cannot speak, since Viscount Bindon is unknown to me."

"Did not you sign the betrothal contract, papa?"

"I did indeed. But in saying that Viscount Bindon is unknown to me, I meant just that. He was simply Lord Thomas Howard when I saw him then. In his fourteenth summer, he was not of an age when one might make a fair assessment. I saw him as a shy, rather withdrawn youth who resembled his flamboyant elder brother, the Earl of Surrey, only in appearance."

"The Earl of Surrey is called *The Poet Earl,* is he not?" asked Catherine with interest.

"He is so called, and is regarded by many as the greatest living poet. His lady is Frances, daughter to the Earl of Oxford – they are idyllically happy, it is said. The Duke's only daughter, Mary, was the child bride of the Duke of Richmond, King Henry's bastard."

"The Duke of Richmond is dead, is he not?"

"He is indeed. He died, alas, before the marriage with Lady Mary had been consummated." Lord Dorset hesitated as if weighing his words carefully before he continued. "Know you what consummation means, Catherine?"

"I do, papa," nodded Catherine. "My governess has spoken of it. It means that, once a marriage has been blessed by Holy

Church, husband and wife may share the same bed and God will bless them with children. I confess I know not how …"

"That is well," hastily interposed Lord Dorset. "I am glad to hear that your governess has enlightened you as to consummation and what will be expected of you."

"Papa, I am not sure as to …"

"Have patience, daughter," put in Lord Dorset. "When the time comes, it will be your new-wedded lord's duty and privilege to enlighten you more fully."

Two

Two weeks and three days later, Catherine sat by a brightly burning fire in the large, sumptuously furnished chamber that had been allotted to her at Kenninghall Palace. Forlorn and homesick, she thought back to the days that had preceded her departure from Sackville.

The time had passed all too quickly. When the dreaded day had arrived, pale-faced and making a valiant effort to hold back her tears, she had bade farewell to her beloved family. Then, escorted by men wearing the Sackville livery and with Brigid by her side, she had set forth on the long journey to Norfolk.

On reaching the iron gates at the end of the driveway, she had drawn rein for a moment and turned in her saddle to look back at the magnificent mansion that had been her home all her life. But a last look at Sackville Hall was denied her, for tears had blurred her vision and already it was lost to her.

The journey, with overnight halts at hostelries along the way, had taken three days in all. But to Catherine it had seemed interminable. Journey's end had come in sight quite suddenly when, riding out of woodland on to a large open plain, the tall turrets of Kenninghall could be seen dominating the distant landscape.

Situated on an eminence that sloped gently towards the south, the mansion had been built by the third Duke of Norfolk in the shape of an H. It was largely self-supporting, a mill, slaughter-house, forge and various other out-buildings having been built at a convenient distance from the house, though separated from it by a wide moat. Entrance to the house was by way of a three-arched brick bridge.

Of recent construction and great beauty, Kenninghall had been designed for comfort and luxury, as a family home. As such, it was a striking contrast to Framlingham, the grim Suffolk fortress built by the Duke's ancestors.

A family home? There had been little evidence of that as Catherine and her entourage had ridden into the courtyard. There had been servants a-plenty – but the Howard family themselves had been conspicuously absent.

Escorted to her chamber by one of the upper servants and with Brigid following, she had been shown every considera-tion. She had welcomed the opportunity for rest and refreshment after the exhausting journey, and had bade Brigid take rest in the small adjoining chamber provided for her.

But several hours had elapsed and, though it was by then early evening, still Catherine had seen none save the servants. I feel like a traveller lost in some foreign land, she thought. No member of the Howard family was here to greet me, and yet clearly my arrival was expected. Why then so cold a reception?

There came a knock on the door at that point and, as if her question had been heard, a young lady entered.

Simply but expensively dressed in a gown of blue silk, the newcomer was strikingly handsome, although the beauty of her dark eyes and long dark hair was marred by the somewhat petulant line of her mouth.

"I am Mary, Duchess of Richmond," said the newcomer, coming forward to embrace Catherine. "Welcome to Kenninghall, my lady. My lord father bade me convey his regret that he and my brother were unable to be here to greet you on your arrival. He had urgent business to attend to – if all goes well, he will return upon the morrow."

"It is a pleasure to make your acquaintance, my lady," said Catherine. "I understand about His Grace's absence, and look forward to meeting him upon the morrow."

"I trust you have recovered from the rigours of your journey. I always find travelling so boring and exhausting – though it does depend of course on what or who is waiting for one at journey's end."

"Quite so," agreed Catherine whole-heartedly. "The

journey from Dorset was not too wearisome, but I have never left Dorset before and feel like a traveller in a foreign land."

"If there is anything you need you have only to ask," Mary assured her. "There is an abundance of servants to do your bidding – my lord father employs four hundred to staff Kenninghall and Framlingham."

"My personal maid will be returning to Dorset upon the morrow," Catherine said with a carelessness that would have deceived no one – and certainly not Mary.

"Your last link with Sackville?" asked Mary on a slightly mocking note. "Have no fear! Mistress Holland has appointed a girl by the name of Lucy as your new maid – I will send her to you when I leave."

"Mistress Holland?"

Mary's tinkling laughter did nothing to lessen Catherine's uneasiness.

"Methought all England had heard of Bess Holland!" she said.

"She is famous?" asked Catherine.

"One could say that, I suppose," chuckled Mary. "Notorious might be a better word! Did no one tell you of Kenninghall's dark secret? Nay, I can see from your expression they did not. Suffice it to say for the present that Bess Holland is in sole charge of the domestic arrangements here at Kenninghall."

"Oh, I see," said Catherine. "Mistress Holland is the housekeeper."

"In fact she is rather more than the housekeeper," said Mary obscurely. "Anyway, you will learn more of Bess Holland later on I dare say. Meanwhile, if you lack for aught that servants can provide, Bess Holland will arrange it for you. She will be along later to introduce herself. You must still be weary from your journey, so I will leave you now. Perchance we can talk together again upon the morrow."

"I would like that," smiled Catherine.

"I hope you will be happy here, Catherine, and that we shall be friends – I have always wanted a sister."

* * *

Bess Holland was in no way the type of woman Catherine had expected. She had pictured her as a typical housekeeper: an austere woman of middle years who wore high necked black gowns and had a large bunch of keys, the hallmark of her office, attached to her waist-belt.

Bess Holland certainly wore black and was probably in her middle years, and she did indeed carry a large bunch of keys. But there the prototype of a typical housekeeper ended.

Her gown was of black velvet, and expertly fashioned to display her voluptuous curves to advantage. Her features clearly indicated her peasant origin, her mouth and eyes suggesting a blatant sensuality, and she wore an abundance of beautiful jewellery that was enhanced by the dark gown.

"Welcome to Kenninghall, my lady," she said in a warm, husky voice, and with the briefest of curtseys. "I am Elizabeth Holland, and am responsible to His Grace for the smooth running of his household. I trust you have found everything to your liking."

"All my needs have been met, Mistress Holland, and this chamber is quite beautiful," said Catherine with sincerity. "I have all I require."

"Then you are the only member of the Howard family who has," chuckled Bess. "I trust you will be able to say as much in six months' time!"

"Why do you say that?"

"This, my lady, is not a happy household – as you will discover, alas," explained Bess. "Let us hope your presence here will improve the situation."

"I fail to understand you, Mistress Holland," Catherine said coldly, baffled by the plain speaking of a housekeeper who seemed to regard herself as an equal.

"You will understand soon enough, my lady," Bess told her. "When Lady Frances first came here as the Earl of Surrey's bride, she had hopes of reforming the household. But she is a gentle lady, reserved and kindly, and such a one is no match for Kenninghall. That was why the Earl built Mount Surrey a few miles distant – that he and Lady Frances could set up home elsewhere."

"Mount Surrey is a magnificent mansion by all accounts," said Catherine.

"It is indeed," agreed Bess. "But one wonders whether Lady Frances has regrets about the move."

"Why do you say that, Mistress Holland?" Catherine could not resist the question.

"No sooner had she and the Earl taken possession of their new home, than he was away to the French wars," explained Bess. "Two years he was away, first as second in command to the Duke his father, and then in sole command. He only returned to England in March. Still, the Countess has her children – which is more than can be said of many of us."

"You are married then, Mistress Holland?" asked Catherine innocently.

Bess laughed mockingly. "Married? What a question! You must have been carefully screened from scandal down there in Dorset. I thought the world and his wife had heard of Bess Holland and her goings-on!"

Not liking the turn the interview had taken, Catherine remained silent for a few moments. Mistress Holland is a servant, albeit an upper servant, she thought, and I must discourage gossip and familiarity – papa would expect it of me. I fear that papa would not greatly approve of Mistress Holland.

"I am a little tired, Mistress Holland," she said.

"Of course, my lady, and I must not weary you further with my chatter."

"Oh, I did not mean to ..."

"Just ring if there is anything at all you require, my lady," interposed Bess firmly. "Your former maid will be returning to Sackville in the morning, I understand. I trust you will find Lucy satisfactory – she is a local lass and is very anxious to please."

"Thank you, Mistress Holland."

"I shall return here in the morning – at eleven o'clock if that suits you." Bess's voice was brisk. "You can tell me then if you have any instructions for me."

"At what hour is His Grace expected home?" Catherine tried, not too successfully, to make the enquiry sound casual.

"Late afternoon – in time for supper, he said," Bess told her. "Doubtless you are anxious to renew your acquaintance with Viscount Bindon – Lord Thomas, as he is called in the household."

"Renew my acquaintance?" Catherine smiled wanly. "Our marriage was contracted by our parents when I was three years of age. Lord Thomas and I have never met."

"Time will remedy that omission," smiled Bess, registering Catherine's lack of enthusiasm with interest. "Lord Thomas is not an easy gentleman to know, it must be admitted, but doubtless he's as eager for a bedding as the next man!"

"Mistress Holland, I really do not think ..." Catherine was annoyed to find herself blushing.

"I bid you a good night, my lady," interposed Bess, noting Catherine's confusion. "I expect you are feeling a trifle forlorn here, away from your family, but you will like Kenninghall – once you know your way around."

"Good-night, Mistress Holland," said Catherine with an air of unconcern she was far from feeling. "Pray have no fears on my account. I am very adaptable and am already beginning to feel at home here."

* * *

Despite her brave words, Catherine remained awake for a long time after she had retired. She lay in the great canopied bed, seeing the beauty of her surroundings through a mist of tears. The bed was of walnut, and its tester was made of crimson velvet embroidered with gold. The five bedcurtains were of crimson silk, and the counterpane, of crimson taffeta, displayed the Howard coat of arms embroidered in gold thread.

The coat of arms seemed like an affront to Catherine in her misery. 'Tis as if I have been despatched and delivered to this unwelcoming house, she thought to herself, and lie here now like a package labelled with the Howard arms. 'Tis as if already I belong to the Howard family, body and soul.

Homesickness overwhelmed her and she no longer tried to

hold back her tears. Brigid having been assigned a pallet bed in the ante-chamber, she was quite alone and was thankful that there was no one to witness her wretchedness.

She was many miles distant from her beloved family, and her gentle heart needed reassurance and love. It seemed to her that the world she had known had abandoned her, and that she was alone in an unknown land, in hostile unfamiliar territory.

What is going on at Sackville Hall now? she wondered. Will father be sitting reading by the hearth until the early hours as is his wont? Dear papa! He pretended he was resigned to my departure, that he saw it as a step towards a glorious future for me. But I was not deceived. I saw his expression as he embraced me in farewell. I heard the emotion in his voice and recognised his reluctance to let me go.

What of my brother Edward, who is two years older than I and is soon to be married? He is more fortunate than I, she thought, for he and his bride will make their home at Sackville. What of my sisters? How are Cecily and Margaret, and Ann who is only eight years old, faring without me? Are they too lying in bed crying at our separation? Did Drumcullen, my grey stallion, snort with disapproval when one of the grooms, instead of myself, went to the stables to exercise him on the past three mornings? Are my little lapdogs, Tootsie and Sweetie, pining for me?

Will I ever see my loved ones again? she asked herself. Not, I think, as Catherine Sackville. If I one day return to Sackville Hall, I shall be accompanied by my husband. I shall be Lady Catherine Howard, Viscountess Bindon.

"My husband!" she said softly to herself. How strange those words sound on my lips! Somewhere out there in that unknown, hostile world, there is a gentleman by the name of Thomas Howard who is my betrothed. What is he like? Why was he not here to welcome me? Was my arrival of small importance to him?

Will he love me? she wondered miserably. Will he be kind and patient with me? I know nothing of the world – and very little of marriage. *'Twill be your new husband's duty and privilege, when the time comes, to teach you,* papa said.

But what if Thomas Howard is unpleasing to me? What if I am unpleasing to him? What if he is impatient and unkind – cruel to me even? To whom in this vast unfriendly mansion, peopled by strangers, would I turn for solace?

Three

The day that followed was dull and rainy, and did nothing to enliven Catherine's spirits. She bade a mutually tearful farewell to Brigid, to dear Brigid whose warm motherliness had helped to comfort Catherine and her sisters after the death of their mother.

"Oh Brigid, I wish you could stay!" Catherine said. "I know you and Silas are to be wed, and far be it from me to begrudge you your chance of happiness, but if only you could remain here for a few weeks."

"Hush, lovey!" said Brigid, tears coursing down her cheeks. "'Tis best this way. Each household has its own arrangements, its own way of liking things done, and every mistress prefers to choose her servants."

"Kenninghall has no mistress," Catherine pointed out. "The Duke and his lady wife have been estranged, and have kept separate households, for many years past."

"Hearken to me, lovey," Brigid said, with sudden determination. "I'll say this much before I go, so's you'll know where you stand. The Duke and Duchess live separate lives, as you said. Could one of her noble lineage – she's a descendant of King Edward III and John of Gaunt, 'tis said – tolerate the open presence of her husband's mistress in her household? What lawful wife, mother of her husband's children, would take second place to a harlot?"

"A harlot? That is a wicked word, Brigid, and I have not heard it on your lips before."

"For once, my dove, your Brigid is going to speak plainly. Bess Holland is the Duke's mistress and, as such, rules his

27

household. She was once the Duchess's laundress, as is well known, but she beguiled the Duke and she's remained his mistress these twenty-seven years past."

"But I do not understand," Catherine said in puzzlement. "If a man has a wife, why would he want a mistress?"

"You're too young and innocent as yet to understand that, lovey," Brigid told her. "But be wary of Bess Holland – that's my advice to you."

"But I am to marry Viscount Bindon. What has his father's mistress to do with me?"

"Viscount Bindon – or Lord Thomas as he is called here – does as his father tells him," explained Brigid. "That's what's said among the servants – I've kept my eyes and ears well open during the short while I've been here."

"The servants could well be mistaken," pointed out Catherine, though her voice lacked conviction.

"Why else didn't His Lordship insist on being here to greet you yesterday?" demanded Brigid. "The Duke is in his seventy-second year, but he's as spry as ever, it seems. He's clever and cunning as a fox, they say, and only Bess Holland holds the key to his mind."

"The Duke is very old," mused Catherine. "He is many years senior to papa, and yet his children, are only in their twenties."

"He was first married to Anne, daughter of Edward IV, as your lord father will have told you. No offspring of that marriage survived and, by the time his first Duchess died and the Duke was free to marry again, he was already approaching his middle years."

"Oh, Brigid, in the short time I have been at Kenninghall, I have learned much about the family into which I must marry," complained Catherine. "All I have heard has increased my uneasiness, and seemed to widen the gulf between the Howard family and myself. Why did not papa tell me that the Duke's household is ruled by a harlot?"

"Because he didn't wish to worry you needlessly, I expect," Brigid told her. "As your lord father sees it, you are to become the bride of the most eligible bachelor in England, and that will make up for less agreeable aspects of your marriage. As I see it, a bit of knowledge can be mighty useful at times – remember, lovey, I'm only a servant, and we servants ofttimes see things differently from the gentry. Forewarned is forearmed, as is said, and it seems to me it won't do any harm for you to know a little of your husband-to-be's background."

"Mistress Holland told me that Lord Thomas is a difficult gentleman to know," Catherine said nervously. "What did she mean, Brigid?"

"I expect she meant that she'd never managed to know him," said Brigid darkly. "But don't trouble your pretty head about that. Lord Thomas is reserved, they say, unlike his brother, the Earl of Surrey. But remember, little mistress, that this couldn't have been a happy household for children to grow up in – I daresay Lord Thomas, as well as his brother and sister, has been affected by his parents' unhappy marriage. The Earl of Surrey, they say, though wild and headstrong, is happily married. Please God the same will be said of Lord Thomas's marriage."

"Amen to that," agreed Catherine fervently. "Oh, Brigid, will I ever see you again?"

"Who knows what lies ahead for any of us, little mistress?" Brigid's voice was practical.

"As soon as I have settled down here and am well acquainted with Lord Thomas, I shall persuade him to take me on a visit to Sackville," said Catherine, in an attempt to raise her own spirits. "Would not that be wonderful, Brigid?"

"It would," agreed Brigid. "It would indeed. But don't depend on it, little mistress. Don't depend on it – that's Brigid's advice to you. Now, I'll just get my things together, for the men-at-arms will be mounting up in a few minutes and I don't want to cause a delay."

* * *

Catherine awoke from a deep sleep on the morning after Brigid's departure, and could not for a few moments recall where she was. At first she imagined herself to be in her familiar chamber at Sackville, the one she had shared with her fourteen year old sister Cecily.

But then she recalled where she was and, drawing aside one of the bedcurtains, she climbed out of the bed and went lightly over to the tall window. Shivering with the cold, she nevertheless knelt on the velvet-cushioned window seat and looked out. It was a bright, though chilly, morning, and the golden October sunlight was a welcome contrast to the sunless gloom of the previous day.

After Brigid's departure, the previous day had passed slowly and uneventfully for Catherine. Bess Holland had paid her a brief, formal visit, but she had seen no one else but the servants. Her homesickness and despondency increased by Brigid's departure, she had retired early and thankfully to bed. Perchance, she had told herself as she drifted into sleep, things will look brighter upon the morrow ...

She turned from the window, rang the bell, and climbed back into the still-warm bed. Almost immediately her new maid entered the chamber.

"Good morning, my lady," she curtseyed. "I trust you slept well."

"I did indeed, Lucy," smiled Catherine.

"I'll have them bring your breakfast to you on a tray, my lady," said Lucy, busying herself with drawing back the curtains. "After breakfast, I expect you'll wish to remain here in your chamber nice and cosy, so I'll summon servants to replenish the fire. Lady Mary always remains in her chamber till lunch-time."

"I shall get dressed after breakfast, Lucy, and then I mean to have a good look at Kenninghall and try to find my way around," Catherine told her.

"I'm not sure if Mistress Holland would like that, my lady. Anyway, I'll tell her what you plan to do, and perchance she'll show you round herself. Or maybe, if you wait till this afternoon, Lady Mary will ..."

"There is no need to mention the matter to Mistress Holland," interposed Catherine.

"Oh, but I must, my lady," said the girl nervously. "She was most particular about that."

"About what?"

"About me telling her what you plan to do, if you've a fancy for leaving your chamber, my lady."

"Say nothing for now, Lucy," Catherine said with a firmness that belied her growing uneasiness. I feel like a prisoner who must not leave her cell unaccompanied! she thought. "I may change my mind. Anyway, I shall have my breakfast now and the servants can see to the fire, and then I shall decide what to do."

Thus it was, bored and resentful, Catherine remained in her chamber for the rest of the morning. She lacked nothing that servants and luxurious surroundings could provide, but her loneliness and homesickness were increasing by the hour.

Lucy unpacked the trunks and travelling bags that Catherine had brought with her, and which contained her trousseau. There was her white bridal gown, gowns of velvet and damask, flounced petticoats, nightgowns skilfully embroidered and trimmed lavishly with lace, and negligées of velvet, their edges trimmed with white fur.

"Mistress Holland told me that you're to be married in three months' time," Lucy said as she unpacked the trunks and, in accordance with Catherine's instructions, placed the garments in the hanging closet that adjoined the chamber. "'Tis ever so exciting, my lady, to have a real bride here at Kenninghall."

"In truth, I have been married since I was three years old – in the eyes of the law," sighed Catherine. "And yet I have not once set eyes on my betrothed. Is not that strange?"

Lucy shrugged. "'Tis the way with gentry, my lady," she said practically.

"I am told that His Grace and Lord Thomas will be returning to Kenninghall later today," Catherine said carelessly. "So I must give thought to which gown I shall wear for my first meeting with my lord."

* * *

At Lady Mary's invitation, Catherine had lunch with her in the private apartment she occupied in the household.

"So you are to meet your betrothed at last," Lady Mary said, as soon as they had finished lunch and the servants had departed. "I pray you will be more fortunate than I. I was sixteen, the age you are now, when I became a widow – and for the past eleven years I have remained a widow who was never truly a wife!"

"How sad it is that you lost your husband so soon!" said Catherine.

Mary shrugged. "The Duke of Richmond was all but a stranger to me – in much the same way that my brother is a stranger to you. My grief at his passing was only for what might have been, for many believed that, had he lived, Henry of Richmond would one day have become King of England – His Majesty was already planning to legitimise him."

"And then you would have become Queen," said Catherine. "Then you truly lost much when you lost your husband."

"That is all in the past now," Mary said carelessly. "I look only to the future – as you are surely doing at the present time."

"The future?" Catherine's voice expressed her uneasiness. "The future is a closed book at present."

"The future is always a closed book," said Mary, but then she smiled mischievously. "You are very pretty, Catherine. 'Tis a good thing my brother, Henry of Surrey, is away from home just now, or he would have ridden post-haste from Mount Surrey to take a look at his future sister-in-law."

"Would that matter?" asked Catherine.

"Brother Henry is inclined to overshadow poor Thomas," Mary explained lightly. "It has always been thus. When we were children, Henry was always the leader in our escapades. The ladies find it difficult to resist Henry of Surrey's charm. Frances, poor fool, thinks the sun shines out of his eyes! He is frequently away from home on missions for the King – as well as on those occasions when some rash enterprise has landed him in the Tower. That has happened more than once, but always the King pardons him and heaps fresh honours on him. Even His Majesty is not impervious to Henry's charm: he remembers Henry of Surrey's friendship with his bastard, Henry of Richmond – Lancelot and Galahad, he called them!"

"Then Lady Frances sees little of her husband," said Catherine in surprise. "Rumour has it that the Earl and Countess of Surrey are devoted to each other."

"There is truth in the rumour – to some extent," admitted Mary grudgingly. "Frances has given my brother four children, and is again with child, but for each of her confinements Henry has been many miles from home, in Scotland or France – or even in the Tower! Does Frances complain? Never. I see her as something of a doormat. All the same, Henry does dote on her, and she on him – such a fact never fails to surprise me, for my brother has had more than his fair share of amorous intrigues."

"You speak much of the Earl of Surrey," Catherine said curiously, "but little of your other brother. Why so?"

"There is much to say of Henry, but little to say of Thomas," Mary told her. "As I said, Thomas is overshadowed by Henry when they are together."

"You favour your elder brother?"

"On the contrary. I hate him." Mary's voice was cool, and Catherine wondered for an instant if she were serious.

"You would have me believe that you hate your own brother?" Catherine asked, in astonishment. "How could that be, my lady?"

"I hate Henry of Surrey just as I hate my lord father – and for the same reason," insisted Mary. "I am all but a prisoner here in Norfolk. My father has kept me always as his pawn, one who will eventually be sold to the highest bidder, while I have had no other choice than to spend the days and years of my widowhood either in attendance on the Queen at Court, or in boredom and loneliness here at Kenninghall. To my father and Henry, my chastity is necessary to their political intrigues. My father sees it as a useful adjunct with which to bait the trap whilst he waits for the highest bidder in the marriage market.

When my father does arrive at a decision and agreement is reached, my brother decides the gentleman is unsuitable and does his utmost to persuade my father against the match.''

"So that is how it is," said Catherine.

Mary nodded. "That is how it is. My father at one time favoured a match betwixt myself and Sir Thomas Seymour, but Henry put paid to that – that is why I hate him," she explained.

"You had a deep regard for Sir Thomas Seymour?" asked Catherine.

"I have a deep regard for Tom Seymour," Mary admitted. "I know his faults. He is an opportunist and a lecher, he is a Protestant, and is of humble origin – but I love him dearly. Compared with the Howards, everyone is of humble origin, alas!"

"Would you, a Catholic, marry a Protestant then?" asked Catherine.

"I would marry a heathen – if I loved him," Mary said passionately. "My brother prates of family honour, but does family honour warm my bed at night, and provide me with a loving husband and children?"

"Then you would wed Sir Thomas Seymour – against your father's wishes?"

"That is my single-minded ambition." Mary's voice was bitter and self-pitying, Catherine noticed, and suggested a shrewishness that was at odds with her dark-eyed, aristocratic beauty. "But Tom Seymour is disapproved of to such an extent by both my father and brother, that I fear it will not be easy to realize my ambition. But I am my mother's child, thanks be to God: I shall not give in without a fight. I am also a Howard, which means that I too can lay plans coolly and cunningly. Somehow I shall find a means of outwitting my father and my brother. I shall yet achieve my own ends.''

Four

It was nearing dusk when Bess Holland came to Catherine's chamber to inform her that the Duke and Lord Thomas had returned and, at her convenience, would be pleased to greet her in the solar.

"Thank you, Mistress Holland," Catherine said coldly, giving no hint of the sudden quickening of her pulses.

"I shall conduct you to the Long Gallery, my lady," Bess told her. "Later, supper will be served formally in the Great Hall as befits the occasion, though normally, when alone, the family partakes of meals in the parlour, the smaller chamber adjacent to the Hall."

The suggestion that Catherine too was "family" gave her an inexplicable feeling of resentment, but she quelled the hasty retort that rose to her lips.

"Thank you, Mistress Holland," she said instead. "I shall be ready in one hour."

* * *

After careful consideration, Catherine selected one of her new gowns and started to dress with Lucy's willing, though slightly disapproving, assistance.

"What is it, Lucy?" asked Catherine, noticing the girl's uncustomary silence. "Do not you like the gown?"

Lucy gazed at the gown which was of jade green velvet. Though cut with a skill that displayed Catherine's shapely figure to perfection, the gown, with its square neckline and tight bodice, was conventional to the point of simplicity. Its splendour lay in its full hanging sleeves, which had been lavishly and intricately embroidered with gold thread and pearls.

"It is beautiful, my lady," she said. "'Tis only the colour that concerns me."

"The colour?" asked Catherine in surprise. "I like this shade of green and imagined it suited me well."

She turned and, gazing at her reflection in the long mirror, surveyed herself critically. Her light blonde hair – only partially concealed by a french hood of velvet that matched her gown and was trimmed with pearls and gold thread – hung luxuriantly down her back, while her green eyes and the creamy-whiteness of her face and throat were enhanced by the colour of the gown.

"Indeed it does suit you well, my lady," said Lucy. "'Tis just that, in these parts, 'tis said to be unlucky for a maiden to wear green."

"That is just a superstition," said Catherine. "Surely no one truly believes it."

"I'll not wear green before I'm wed," admitted Lucy. "I'd call to mind the rhyme and the occasions when it had spoken truly."

"Tell me this rhyme," insisted Catherine.

"It goes like this, my lady:

'Wear a green kirtle before you be wed
And you'll have no husband to warm your bed
So put on your blue, your russet, or red,
Or still be a maid on the day you're dead'."

Catherine smiled. "It must be a rhyme peculiar to Norfolk – I have certainly not heard it before. Anyway, Lucy, it is mere superstition and I was brought up to believe that a good Catholic is not influenced by superstition. Are not you a Catholic?"

"Of course I am, my lady," Lucy said defensively. "All the same, I'd not seek for trouble by wearing green."

"And I am not pandering to superstition by hearkening to

some old rhyme," said Catherine firmly. "I shall wear the gown if only to prove to you that no possible harm can come from it."

"As you wish, my lady," said Lucy, with the resigned air of one whose words of wisdom had been ignored. "I will fetch your jewel box."

"There is no need, Lucy," said Catherine. "Just bring me the long row of pearls. I shall entwine them twice round my throat – no other jewellery will be necessary, for it would detract from the embellishments on my gown."

In truth, Catherine's air of confidence was misleading. Determined to hide her apprehension even from her maidservant, she was nevertheless a prey to anxiety and doubt.

Will Lord Thomas find me pleasing? was the question uppermost in her mind. Does he like fair-haired maidens? she wondered. Will he consider me too slender – or too plump? Will he disapprove of my green gown? Could there be truth in that old rhyme? Nay, of course not. It is a superstition, no more, and one peculiar to these parts – as Lucy says.

"You look beautiful, my lady," Lucy said admiringly, breaking in on Catherine's reverie. "I'd not have the courage to wear such a colour myself, but no one could deny it suits you. You look like a bride already."

Five

Catherine's cool blonde beauty and air of serenity belied the agitated beating of her heart as, accompanied by a silent Bess Holland, she entered the Long Gallery.

Lady Mary was standing half way along the elegantly furnished chamber, talking animatedly to two gentlemen. At the sound of footsteps in the stone-flagged doorway, all three turned in Catherine's direction, and at once the elder gentleman came towards her, smiling benevolently.

"So this is little Catherine Sackville!" smiled the Duke approvingly, as Catherine made her curtsey. "By my faith, I had no idea that such beauty was blossoming quietly there in Dorset!"

"You are kind, Your Grace," said Catherine.

"I bid you welcome to Norfolk, my lady, and tender my sincere regrets that it was not possible for my son and me to be here to greet you on your arrival," said the Duke, taking her hands in his. "I fear that my son will never forgive me for further delaying his meeting with you. Is not that so, Thomas?"

Lord Thomas had joined his father by this time, and the Duke introduced him.

"This is my son Thomas, Viscount Bindon," he said, and then smiled. "You notice that my son has chosen to ignore my question? Alas, it is as I feared – he refuses to forgive me!"

"It is good to meet you, my lord," Catherine said, curtseying to Lord Thomas. "We have waited many years for this meeting."

"It is indeed good to meet you, my lady," Lord Thomas said gravely, with a formal bow.

"Pray be seated, my lady," said the Duke, indicating a high-backed velvet-cushioned chair by the fire. "My son and I will be seated also, for we owe you an explanation as to the reason for our absence. My daughter will join us later for supper."

"But, my lord ..." Mary started to protest.

"You mentioned a moment ago that you had a small matter to attend to before supper," said the Duke urbanely. "Pray do not let us detain you."

Not troubling to hide her annoyance but not daring to make further protest, Mary flounced angrily from the chamber.

"My elder son, the Earl of Surrey, was summoned to London in August for the reception of De la Garde, the new French ambassador," explained the Duke. "He became involved in a certain political intrigue – I will not trouble you with the details, my dear – which placed him at some – er – disadvantage at Court. It was therefore necessary that his brother and I should go to London and discover for ourselves what was toward. All is now well, I am glad to say. My son returned with us from London and is now at Mount Surrey."

"I am glad to hear it, Your Grace," said Catherine, "and I greatly appreciate your telling me the reason for your absence."

"Pray tell us of yourself, my lady." The Duke's manner was warm and genial, and it was impossible for Catherine to see him as the cunning opportunist his enemies proclaimed him to be. "I feel sure that my son is far more interested in you, than in the intrigues of his brother. Is it not so, Thomas?"

Lord Thomas nodded gravely. "That is so, my lord," he said.

Catherine looked at him, taking in the tall, well-made figure, the aristocratic features, and the beautiful dark eyes he had inherited from his Plantagenet forebears.

Thomas Howard was undeniably handsome, but his expression was grave and his manner reserved. Plainly it was as Bess Holland had said: Thomas Howard was not an easy man to know.

"There is little enough to tell, Your Grace," she said shyly.

"I have lived a very dull life at Sackville Hall and have never been away from Dorsetshire before in my whole life."

It was unfortunate that Mary, clearly banished by her father for reasons best known to himself, chose that moment to return to the Long Gallery.

"And now you have come to live a very dull life at Kenninghall Palace, and will hardly ever be away from Norfolk again in your whole life," she said, still smarting from the Duke's humiliating dismissal.

"My daughter affects to be something of a wit, my lady," said the Duke, glancing coldly at Mary. "Pray take no notice of her. The fault is partially mine, alas – being my only daughter, she was over indulged in her youth. I beg you take warning from that, my dear, and resolve that, should you be blessed with a daughter, you will not make the same mistake as myself."

Blushing at the reference to her unborn children, Catherine was painfully conscious of Lord Thomas's gaze upon her. But when, a few moments later, she covertly glanced in his direction, he removed his gaze and looked instead at the leaping flames in the hearth, as if he found them a deal more interesting than his bride-to-be.

"Really, father ..." Mary had started to protest, to be blandly interrupted by the Duke.

"You must meet my other son, Henry of Surrey," he said to Catherine. "He and his Countess, Lady Frances, are a devoted couple. You and Frances will get on well together. She is a real charmer and I love her dearly – there is nothing of the shrew in her!"

Aware that the last remark had been in reference to herself, Mary smiled scornfully.

"I suppose dear Frances is in raptures now that my wandering brother has returned," she said.

"You are right there, daughter," agreed the Duke. "It did my old heart good to see Henry and Frances reunited – one seldom sees such happiness in a marriage."

As if by way of changing the subject, Lord Thomas addressed himself to Catherine.

"And how do you like Kenninghall, my lady?" he asked.

"I confess it frightens me a little, my lord," admitted Catherine. "It is so large, like a maze, and I fear to lose myself if I venture far from my chamber alone."

"You will soon learn to find your way about," Lord Thomas told her. "Kenninghall is like all large houses in that it shares the infallible rule for finding one's way around. Study it from the outside, and from each aspect. That way, you will see it as a whole – and the secret of the maze will be yours."

"My son is right," agreed the Duke. "My son is usually right."

"Anyway, my lady, I myself shall count it a privilege to show you around Kenninghall," said Lord Thomas courteously. "I trust that in time it will be not merely a house, but also a home to you."

Six

True to his word, Lord Thomas took Catherine on a tour of the house on the following afternoon. He showed her all the main halls and chambers, and told her the origins of many of the priceless tapestries that covered the walls, as well as the colourful histories of his forebears whose faces gazed down somewhat dauntingly from the portraits in the picture gallery.

A passageway led from the main entrance to a large dining-chamber, at the further end of which was a door that gave entrance to a cloister. The cloister, overlooking a flower-garden that had been constructed within the walls of the moat, was terminated by a series of spacious kitchens with long oaken tables.

On the other side of the main entrance there was a chapel, and beyond this a door into the Great Hall. This lofty and imposing chamber contained a magnificent stone fireplace which was elaborately carved with the Howard coat of arms, stained glass windows of great beauty, and priceless tapestries. At one end of the Hall a door in the middle of a screen of brown wainscot led through to the buttery.

"My youngest sister, Ann, used to insist when she was small that a buttery is where butter is made," smiled Catherine at this point. "Butter is churned in the dairy, we used to tell her, and the buttery is where the wine butts are stored."

"I expect you miss your sisters," remarked Lord Thomas.

"I do indeed," nodded Catherine. "Just mentioning Ann has given me a wave of homesickness. Alas, you must think me very foolish!"

"Not at all, my lady," he assured her. "'Tis natural that you should miss your family. I trust that in time you will come to regard us as your family."

"Kenninghall is truly beautiful, my lord, and much bigger than Sackville," Catherine told him. "I am sure I shall never find my way around on my own."

"You will get used to finding your way around sooner than you think," he assured her. "Beneath these apartments are the cellars."

"They lie close to the moat, my lord."

"They are dry and well-ventilated nevertheless, being well vaulted with brick." He smiled. "You will have to take my word for that, my lady – for there is plenty else to see for one day!"

He led her next to an inner hall, whence two wrought iron staircases of great splendour swept upwards to the galleries and chambers above.

"I remember an occasion several years ago when my brother and I brought down a full measure of our lord father's wrath when, each of us taking a flight, we raced our horses up these stairs," chuckled Lord Thomas as they made their way to the top. "Poor Henry received most of the blame for the damage we caused, for father was convinced he was the ringleader!"

"As he was?" asked Catherine.

"As he was," admitted Lord Thomas.

They had reached the top of the staircase by this time and Catherine looked around with interest.

"The family's apartments are here and are built above the gateway chapel and the Great Hall," Lord Thomas told her. "The remainder of this first storey is given over to smaller bedchambers and a still-room."

"Since my mother died, the still-room at Sackville has remained locked and only my lord father has a key," Catherine told him. "I suppose he regards it as the prerogative of the lady of the house."

"Mistress Holland holds one of the keys to the still-room here, just as she holds the keys to the rest of the house," said Lord Thomas.

"But she is a housekeeper," said Catherine in surprise, "and would naturally have charge of the keys. But the still-room is different – the lady of the house maintains it for her own use."

"Alas, since my lady mother left Kenninghall, there has been no lady of the house," Lord Thomas said sadly.

"My mother used to distil waters and cordials, as well as herbal potions and medicaments for the household, and herbs for the cooking pots. Sometimes as a special treat, when I was small, she would let me go and watch her."

"Here is something I especially wished to show you," said Lord Thomas, unlocking the door of a small closet that was contiguous to one of the main bedchambers. "Pray take a look inside, my lady."

Catherine stepped over the threshold and her face lit up with pleasure as she looked around the tiny wainscoted chamber. No more than seven feet square, its ceiling was decorated with gold, while the wooden panels on three sides were embellished with various religious emblems and mottoes, and the fourth panel bore an exquisite tapestry depicting the Annunciation. A prie-dieu, cushioned with velvet and inlaid with gold, stood in front of the tapestry.

"It is beautiful," said Catherine rapturously, "so very beautiful. It is an oratory, is it not?"

Lord Thomas nodded. "It is, as you say, an oratory."

"To whom does it belong, my lord?"

"It will become yours, if you so wish it, on the day we wed," he told her. "Originally, my brother designed it as a surprise for Frances. But before it was completed, he and Frances moved to Mount Surrey and I decided to have it made ready for you. The chamber adjoining will be our bedchamber."

"This is one of the most beautiful things I have ever seen, my lord," Catherine said softly. "It is so small and yet quite complete – even to the tiny window of stained glass. I know not what to say, or how to thank you, my lord."

He smiled briefly at her pleasure and then turned away, waiting for her to precede him through the doorway.

"I am glad you like it," was all he said, as he followed her from the closet and re-locked the door.

"Would you like to see something of the gardens, my lady?"

he asked then. "I see you have brought a warm cloak with you and it is a pleasant enough afternoon."

"I would be delighted to see the gardens, my lord," said Catherine. "The gardens at Kenninghall are renowned for their beauty, I am told. I did venture forth for a few minutes yesterday, but I was fearful of losing my bearings and then it started to rain, so I gave up the idea."

"I trust we shall meet with better fortune today."

"The walls are built of timber and plaster, are they not, my lord?"

"That is so."

"And yet I have noticed that when the sun is shining, they show a most striking effect."

"How so?"

"They sparkle in the sunlight – almost as if they were set with precious stones."

Lord Thomas smiled. "My lord father will be pleased to hear that you have noticed the walls – he takes a great pride in their beauty," he said.

"And rightly so, my lord." Catherine looked at him uncertainly. "May one enquire as to their secret?"

"The plaster is made of hair and coarse sand, and abounds with small stones," Lord Thomas explained. "The outer layer was thickly stuck, whilst still wet, with fragments of glass."

"The result is quite beautiful, my lord – the more so in sunlight."

"And by moonlight also," Lord Thomas told her. "Perchance one evening I shall have the pleasure of showing you the effect by moonlight."

They had reached the gardens by this time and Catherine had fastened her cloak against the sudden chill in the air.

The banks of the moat were planted with yews and variegated hollies, and a short distance beyond there was a terrace that commanded a fine woodland prospect.

Looking down from the terrace, Catherine could see orchards and gardens in abundance.

"I can see a large fish pond," said Catherine excitedly. "Or is it two fish ponds?"

"There are in fact five fish ponds, linked one to the other," explained Lord Thomas. "They are built on the gentle declivity of a hill and run one into another, the upper one being fed by a natural spring."

"There is a very fine park to one side of the woodland, my lord."

"That contains the warrener's lodge," Lord Thomas told her, "and is let to the warrener together with the dairy farm. We have a large number of warrens which make it a profitable occupation."

"Why so, my lord?"

"Coney fur is much used for clothing, as you know. The black skins of the coney fetch a higher price than the carcases."

"You surprise me, my lord," said Catherine.

"I was talking with the warrener the other day and he told me that whilst the carcases sell at 2½d. apiece, the skins can fetch as much as 6d."

* * *

Lord Thomas was kind, considerate and courteous. There was no doubt of that. But when Catherine returned to her chamber after her conducted tour, she was far better acquainted with Kenninghall, but no better acquainted with Thomas Howard.

She was baffled and a trifle piqued by his seeming coldness towards her. Possessed of the same tall build and noble brow as his Plantagenet ancestors, Lord Thomas's dark eyes were unfathomable and suggested a mystery and aloofness that both intrigued and troubled her.

Perchance he is disappointed with me, she said to herself, and is no better pleased with my arrival here than am I myself.

He is polite and considerate, but doubtless he regards such attributes as a duty.

What of my feelings for him? How can I answer such a question, even to myself? He is still a stranger. He is no less a stranger than he has always been, than before I set forth from Sackville Hall. But I must be patient. When we have had more time to get to know one another, perchance his attitude towards me will change.

In fact Catherine was to see little of Lord Thomas or his father during the week that followed their first meeting. The Duke owned vast estates in both Norfolk and Suffolk and, though notorious at Court for his political intrigues and double-dealing, was held in affection by the tenant farmers and peasants of his own county.

Determined to maintain his position as England's premier duke and leading Catholic, the Duke was of necessity frequently absent from home. The greatest soldier of his era, still he led the King's armies into battle when the need arose until, peace prevailing, he returned to Court and used a similar skill and strategy to win his political battles.

Not sharing his father's love of soldiering and intrigue, Lord Thomas was happy to deputise for him during his long absences from home. He issued instructions to bailiffs and stewards, and rode many miles each day, hearing complaints and making judgements, and offering advice to farmer and peasant alike. He knew every person on the estate by name and, though he lacked the bonhomie of his father, he was trusted and respected by all.

Thus it was that, his duties neglected by his enforced visit to Court, Lord Thomas had much to occupy him on his return.

Catherine was therefore left to her own devices. Forlorn and imagining that her husband-to-be had rejected her, she remained mostly in her chamber, feeling more like a prisoner than ever. That she was in fact free to wander through the other chambers and passageways of Kenninghall at will made little difference: whenever she did so, always she found Bess Holland at her side. Informed no doubt by one of the servants of Catherine's movements, Bess was immediately on the scene; and, pleasant and helpful though she seemed on the surface, Catherine nevertheless sensed her hostility.

From time to time Mary, bored and waspish, came to Catherine's chamber to talk to her. Wary of her mockery and caustic remarks, Catherine was never entirely happy in Mary's company, but she listened enthralled to Mary's accounts of life at Court and her own romantic attachments.

It seemed, from Mary's account, that her life had not been wholly virtuous. She is flirtatious, Catherine thought, and has perchance found herself more than once in a compromising situation. I feel sure there is no more to it than that. Probably she is exaggerating a little to test my reaction, for 'tis certain she is in truth a maiden of virtue.

During one of Mary's visits, about a week after Catherine's first meeting with Lord Thomas, Catherine suddenly resolved to ask Mary of her brother.

"I have seen little of my lord Thomas since his return," she said, with deliberate lightness. "In truth I know him no better than before I came here."

"Tom is not an easy person to know," shrugged Mary.

"He is of a reserved temperament perchance?"

Mary looked thoughtful. "Do you wish to learn the truth about Tom?" she asked.

"Of course," nodded Catherine.

"I am not sure if it is wise ..." Mary paused as if considering the matter. "Promise you will not speak of it to my lord father – or Bess Holland."

"Why would I speak of it to Mistress Holland?" demanded Catherine. "One does not discuss matters of a private nature with servants – even upper servants."

Mary laughed mockingly. "You are a goose, Catherine. You really are a goose – you are just too good to be true! I cannot imagine how you will fare when you are married. Bess Holland has been my father's mistress for twenty-seven years ..."

"I know that," interposed Catherine.

"She tells him everything – everything she wishes him to know, that is!"

"But what has that to do with Lord Thomas?" asked Catherine.

"'Like father, like son!' is a popular saying, is it not?" asked Mary darkly. "You surely must have heard it – even in the wilds of Dorset!"

"What mean you?"

"Well, whilst you it seems were reluctant to leave Sackville

Hall and come here to marry a stranger, Thomas was equally reluctant – for your arrival," explained Mary. "Why else would he not have been here to greet his betrothed?"

"His Grace explained …"

"So His Grace explained!" Mary said, mockingly. "Father's explanations are usually poppycock – you will discover that for yourself sooner or later!"

"Why was your brother reluctant to meet me?" asked Catherine.

"Why do you think, my innocent?" asked Mary. "Could there be more than one reason? Nay, of course not – not for one who is my father's son anyway! Thomas is in love with a maiden who lives in one of the villages not far from here. She is the daughter of the village squire and Thomas had hopes of marrying her. But our lord father refused to listen. He reminded Thomas that he was contracted to you. Thomas protested. Of course he protested – and who could blame him? 'Pre-contracts of marriage can be annulled if all parties are willing,' he insisted."

"What did His Grace say to that?" asked Catherine.

"'All parties are not willing – I am not willing!' father retorted." Mary laughed mirthlessly. "And father being father, that to all intents and purposes was the end of the matter."

"I had no idea," said Catherine, white-faced.

"How could you have had?" shrugged Mary. "Thomas is scarcely likely to tell you, and father would skin me alive if he knew I had breathed a word about Tom and the maiden of his heart! But there – 'twas only fair to warn you."

"Then Lord Thomas has no wish to marry me?" asked Catherine in a small voice.

"Oh, Thomas will do his duty, have no fear," said Mary, as if by way of reassurance. "Thomas always does his duty. Now if it were my other brother, Henry of Surrey, it would be another story. Henry goes his own way. Henry would defy anyone – father or even the King himself – in order to get his own way. Thomas obeys father in all things – though he does still meet the squire's daughter whenever opportunity permits.

But he will marry you, never fear, and doubtless he will be a dutiful husband – you will produce a child a year as regular as clockwork!''

"But – but ..." Catherine was on the verge of tears.

"Arranged marriages are always the same," shrugged Mary. "I have yet to hear of a truly happy one."

"My parents were happy and theirs was an arranged match – papa was grief-stricken when poor mama died."

"Always you hear afterwards, when one partner has died, how happy a marriage was," said Mary cynically. "But the grief-stricken widow or widower loses little time in marrying another."

"My father has not," pointed out Catherine. "He has remained a widower. Dear papa honours mama's memory and ..."

"Fiddle-faddle!" interposed Mary. "I expect he keeps his lady-love hidden away in the nearest village, and no one has yet discovered his secret. Men are all the same, Catherine, believe me. You would never dream that Thomas was like that, now would you?"

Catherine shook her head miserably, not trusting herself to speak.

"Of course you would not," agreed Mary. "And that proves my point, does it not?"

"By all accounts, your other brother, the Earl of Surrey, and his Countess are devoted to each other." Catherine reminded her.

"Frances is devoted to Henry – I would not deny that," Mary admitted. "As for Henry – who knows? He is away from home more than he is there and, believe me, he's no monk. Take his poems for instance. Do you know to whom they are dedicated?"

"Nay, I ..."

"To his fair Geraldine!" went on Mary triumphantly. "Not to his fair Frances, you notice! A fine example that is of loyalty and devotion."

Seven

The Earl of Surrey, reunited with his beloved Countess after an absence of several months, spent the weeks that followed his return in connubial bliss and in putting the finishing touches to his magnificent new home, Mount Surrey.

He had spent several hours one day with the French glazier he had brought with him from Calais, discussing the design for the stained glass window that was to beautify one end of the Great Hall.

Sitting with his wife in front of a blazing log fire that evening, Surrey talked enthusiastically of his plans.

"I have decided to make certain alterations to my escutcheon," he said. "I am having the arms of St. Edward the Confessor incorporated in the glass panels."

"Are you entitled to bear the arms of St. Edward, my lord?" asked Frances.

"Of course," nodded Surrey. "Am I not a direct descendant of St. Edward?"

"Would not such an action cause offence to His Majesty?" asked Frances.

"Admittedly since the time of Henry VII, the arms of St. Edward have formed part of the escutcheon of the heir to the throne," said Surrey. "The Tudors hold that right through their Plantagenet blood, as do the Howards also. In altering my escutcheon, I am merely stating that fact ..."

Surrey paused. Frances, for once, appeared not to be listening.

"Do not you agree, my love?" asked Surrey.

Frances gave a start. "Of course I do, my lord," she said hastily.

"You might as well admit it," Surrey said. "You did not hear a single word."

"Oh, but I did, truly I did," insisted Frances. "You were talking of the new window, and the arms of St. Edward, and then – and then ..."

As she floundered into silence, Surrey chuckled.

"And then you lost me," he finished for her. "You have something on your mind this evening, have you not? I noticed it earlier."

Frances sighed. "My mind keeps going back to last night and my first meeting with Catherine Sackville. She has been at Kenninghall for two weeks but that was the first time she had visited Mount Surrey," she said.

"My lord father and Tom have been fully occupied since our return from London," explained Surrey. "And now that you have met Lady Catherine, what is the verdict?"

"My lord, must you express yourself so?" pouted Frances. "You speak as if I invited Lady Catherine here solely to pass judgement on her."

"And you did not?" asked Surrey, his eyes twinkling.

"Of course not," said Frances roundly. "The idea! I merely wished to meet her, to get to know her and – and ..."

"Pass judgement on her?" put in Surrey helpfully.

"Sometimes, Henry of Surrey, I hate you!"

"As long as it is only sometimes," said Surrey carelessly. "Anyway, I am still waiting to hear what you thought of Lady Catherine – and what it is that has caused your mind to wander off on its own all evening!"

"After we had dined, and Lady Catherine and I withdrew to the solar ..." Frances paused and smiled. "I was naturally sorry that Mary had a sore throat – but I could not help feeling glad that only Lady Catherine accompanied your lord father and your brother!"

"Oh, my lord father invented the sore throat," Surrey said lightly. "Mary, I understand, was furious at being left out of things – but father was right of course! He wished you and Lady Catherine to become acquainted without Mary's caustic tongue putting a blight upon the occasion. My lord father hopes that you and Lady Catherine will become friends."

"I think one may safely assume that we are," smiled Frances. "She is beautiful, and has a sweet and gentle disposition. Your brother is truly fortunate, my husband."

"And yet something is troubling you," Surrey said. "Did Lady Catherine confide in you when you retired to the solar? Did she tell you some dark secret?"

Frances looked thoughtful, giving no heed to his banter.

"She is not at all happy at Kenninghall," she said then.

"That does not surprise me," commented Surrey. "You were not happy at Kenninghall – indeed with the situation as it is, it is not easy for anyone to be happy at Kenninghall! But once she and Tom are married, it will be different – Tom will maintain their own household within the palace, or will set up home elsewhere as I have done."

"But it is not just Kenninghall," explained Frances. "In fact, Lady Catherine made no reference to the – er – unconventional arrangements that exist there."

"Then what ails the lass?" asked Surrey. "Why is she unhappy? Is she homesick perchance?"

"Nay, 'tis not just homesickness," Frances said slowly. "You see, my lord, Lady Catherine confided in me and I cannot betray her confidence. We took to each other right away and it was clear to me that she was desperately unhappy. Then, when we were alone in the solar, she could not contain her tears and told me the whole tale."

"Then pray make haste and tell me the whole tale," Surrey said impatiently. "There are better things to do, my love, than sit here all the evening discussing Lady Catherine's tears and fears and confidences!"

"Nay, I promised ..."

"Peter's bones!" exclaimed Surrey. "Must I remind you, my lady, that you also promised to love, honour and obey your lord and master."

"I do love and honour ..."

"'Tis the obedience bit that concerns me at the moment," put in Surrey teasingly. "Since I am ordering you to tell me what ails Lady Catherine, you have no other choice than to obey."

Frances looked relieved. "Of course, if you put it like that ..."

"I most certainly do, my lady."

"Then you leave me no choice, my lord," said Frances with deceptive meekness. "I shall tell you all. Lady Catherine, alas, has discovered the truth."

"And what truth may that be?" asked Surrey, not without a hint of uneasiness.

"The truth about your brother," explained Frances. "Mary told her."

"Mary!" exclaimed Surrey. "I might have guessed she had something to do with this! Pray tell me what was said."

"Mary told Lady Catherine that your brother has formed a deep attachment for a maiden, the daughter of the squire, in one of the nearby villages. Your brother desires to wed the maiden and besought your lord father to arrange for his marriage contract with Lady Catherine to be revoked. Your lord father refused, as was to be expected, and your brother is beside himself with distress."

"And Lady Catherine believed the tale?"

"Of course, my lord," nodded Frances. "Your brother, it seems, though impeccably courteous, keeps Lady Catherine at a distance. His manner towards her is, I gather, cold and withdrawn which – now that she knows the reason – Lady Catherine naturally finds distressing. She has considered writing to her father to ask him to take steps towards having the contract revoked, but she fears it will be of no avail. She has, it seems to me, resigned herself to an unwilling bridegroom and a loveless marriage."

"God's life!" exclaimed Surrey. "Wait till I tell Tom about this!"

"Of course I guessed all along that you already knew of your brother's attachment," said Frances. "But I feel dreadfully sorry for poor Lady Catherine. To be a stranger at Kenninghall is bad enough – I speak with authority – but to be an unwanted stranger must be heartbreaking. She is young and defenceless, my lord, and methinks it would have been kinder to have revoked the marriage contract than to have insisted on the marriage going ahead: your lord father is a hard gentleman."

"You believe the tale about Tom and his secret love?" asked Surrey curiously.

"Of course," said Frances. "How could one not believe it? When Lady Catherine wept and told me of her predicament, I wept also."

"And a good time was had by all," chuckled Surrey.

"'Tis no laughing matter, my lord," Frances said with an unwonted display of anger. "If you had been there and seen poor Lady Catherine's tears …"

"I should have laughed even louder than I am laughing now," said Surrey, going off into great guffaws of laughter. "When I picture you two ladies in the solar, and all that weeping and wailing and gnashing of teeth, I know not how to contain my mirth!"

"Gnashing of teeth indeed!" said Frances. "Since you are determined to treat the matter as a joke and have no care for that poor young lady's feelings, I shall betake myself to my bed and …"

"You do that, my love," interposed Surrey, getting to his feet. "I will try not to disturb you when I return."

"When you return?" asked Frances. "And where, my lord, are you off to at this hour of the night?"

"Kenninghall," said Surrey, trying to repress his mirth.

"But Kenninghall is several miles away, and 'tis close to midnight."

"And what better time could there be for ensuring that my brother will be at home?" demanded Surrey, ringing the bell for a servant and ordering that a horse be made ready for immediate departure.

"At home? He will be at home – and in bed, if you ask me."

"When he hears what I have to say, he will not be in bed for long," Surrey assured her with a grin. "We shall both be rolling around in the aisles with laughter!"

"You are unkind, Henry of Surrey, to treat the matter so lightly," protested Frances. "Speak to your brother if you must, but do not aid and abet him, I beg you. Speak to him of his duty to Lady Catherine."

"Oh, I have no doubt Tom will do his duty in regard to Lady Catherine – when the time comes!"

"You know that is not what I meant, my lord," said Frances reprovingly. "I just do not understand your attitude. I assumed that you would be as shocked as I at Mary's disclosure."

Surrey was suddenly serious. "Believe me, my love, my mirth is in no way induced by Mary's disclosure. But one must learn to play my sister at her own game."

"I do not understand."

"You will – all in good time," Surrey told her. "But first I must speak to Tom. Go to bed, sweeting. I shall be back long before dawn and then perchance I shall tell you the whole story. You could well find yourself laughing over it yet!"

Eight

A few days after Surrey's midnight visit to his former home, Mary sat in her chamber conversing animatedly with Bess Holland.

"Ah me!" she said suddenly. "Here am I, in my twenty-sixth year, a woman who has been a widow for ten years but has never known the embrace of a husband."

"'Tis rumoured at Court that you are somewhat less than virtuous," Bess said quietly.

Mary shrugged. "What if I have consoled myself from time to time with stolen embraces? Surely you, of all people, do not condemn me for that!"

"I have been your lord father's mistress for twenty-seven years – since the year of your birth in fact, my lady," Bess reminded her. "He promised he would marry me as soon as his marriage to the Duchess had been annulled – but I realize now that his promises were no more than moonshine! In truth, I have come to hate him the more with every passing year. My one desire now is to break away from him whilst I still have attraction enough to win a rich husband."

"Why do you speak of this now, Bess?" Mary asked, curiously. "And with such earnestness."

"Perchance we can each help the other to achieve her ambition, my lady."

"My one ambition is to wed Tom Seymour, but I fear there is little hope of that." Mary's voice expressed self-pity. "My father and elder brother are united in their dislike of him. How then could you aid me in my ambition? And how in my turn could I aid you?"

"We must find some means of destroying the power of the Duke and Surrey." Bess's voice was calm, as if she had long given thought to the matter. "That accomplished, you could approach the King, your father-in-law, and ask permission to marry Thomas Seymour."

"You make it sound so simple. But what then, Bess?"

"Once you had achieved your ambition, you would be able to use your improved status to find me a rich husband."

"You speak of my improved status," said Mary a trifle haughtily. "Am I not the only daughter of the highest nobleman in the land – as well as daughter-in-law to the King?"

"Accomplish your ambition and you would be of even higher status," pointed out Bess. "You would have a foot in both camps, so to speak. You would be sister-in-law to His Majesty's late-lamented second wife Jane Seymour, and aunt to the heir to the throne, Prince Edward."

Mary watched her consideringly.

"I can understand, Bess, why you hate my lord father, but what is your complaint against Surrey?" she asked.

"He once tried to seduce me," lied Bess.

"Mother of God! I had no idea!"

"Fearing the Duke's fury if I gave in to his son and he later heard of it, I spurned Surrey's advances. With that, he took his horse-whip to me!"

"God in heaven!" exclaimed Mary aghast. "I see now why you hate him so. But why did you not tell my father of Surrey's ill-treatment of you?"

"Your father would have blamed me," Bess told her, with truth this time. "He'd have accused me of provoking Surrey into seducing me – everyone knows that the Earl is the best loved of His Grace's children."

Designed to provoke Mary to jealousy of her brother, Bess's words had the desired effect.

"Surrey was always father's favourite – and still is," complained Mary. "He uses me merely as an adjunct to his schemes for increasing his power, and he never has known what to make of Thomas. Surrey's flamboyance, his military prowess, even his refusal to be brow-beaten by him – all endear him to father."

"And what of your younger brother?"

"As I said, I believe father never quite knows what to make of Thomas. Whilst he shows obedience to father's whims, in truth he keeps his own counsel. A strange one is Thomas – I doubt whether anyone really knows him."

"He and Surrey are very close."

"Why do you say that?" asked Mary suspiciously. "As if you know something I do not."

"Did you know that Surrey came here to Kenninghall a few nights ago especially to talk to your brother?" asked Bess.

"There is nothing unusual in that. My brothers are very close, as you said – doubtless Surrey had some news to impart to Thomas that could not wait till morning."

"'Twas around midnight. Most of the guards at the gateway had dozed off I gather, and were rudely awakened by a man on horseback who suddenly appeared from the darkness and rode hell for leather over the bridge. By the time one of the guards, rather belatedly I gather, shouted the challenge: 'Who goes there?' Surrey was already riding into the courtyard. 'The King of France' he replied, as he leapt from his saddle, 'come to see if any of you were unable to sleep. But all is well, I see!'"

Mary smiled despite her antagonism towards her brother. "No doubt that caused a few red faces! I wonder what he wanted with Thomas – it certainly was an unconventional hour to call, even for my impetuous brother!"

"I am told –" Bess smiled, making it clear that she had her own spies in the household. "– that Surrey stayed for about an hour. I know not what was said but there was some talk and then a deal of laughter – rollicking laughter, as my informant said."

"I expect Surrey had been spending the evening with some village doxy, and had come to brag to Thomas of his goings-on," Mary said lightly. "Doubtless the matter was of small importance – though I must remember to mention it to dear Frances next time I see her! That might take a little of the shine off his halo!"

"It seems to me the time has come for putting a plan into action," said Bess, determined not to be side-tracked. "Already I have information sufficient to do my lord no small disservice. For twenty-seven years I've listened and waited."

"Listened?"

"Encouraged by my apparent sympathy and understanding, His Grace has treated me as his confidante as well as his mistress," explained Bess. "Lulled with the passing of time into a false sense of security, he has talked to me of his schemes and aspirations as he has talked to no one else in his life."

Mary shivered, shocked in spite of herself by the hatred she saw in the other woman's eyes, by the sudden realization that for more than a quarter of a century Bess Holland had deceived her father into trusting her implicitly.

"You wish me to convey your information to His Majesty?" she asked.

Bess nodded. "I suggest that you seek audience with His Majesty in order to acquaint him with the Duke's traitorous intrigues. At the same time you can inform him of the changes your brother has made in his escutcheon, which imply that the Howards have a stronger claim to the throne than the Tudors."

"I am not sure ..."

"Play your hand wisely, Mary of Richmond, and you can curb the power of both the Duke and Surrey at the same time," interposed Bess, brushing aside Mary's hesitation. "Once that is accomplished, Thomas Seymour will be yours."

Nine

"I am setting forth on my journey to Richmond early upon the morrow," Mary told Lord Thomas a week later. "My own men-at-arms, wearing the Richmond livery, will escort me. I expect to return within the week."

The Duke, on a visit to his Suffolk estate at Framlingham, had been absent from Kenninghall for nearly a week.

"Father made no mention of your going to Richmond," remarked Lord Thomas in surprise.

"Father was not aware of my plans," Mary said haughtily. "I received the summons from the King only an hour or so after father's departure. Was not that unfortunate, my brother?"

"Ill-timed, one might say," said Lord Thomas non-committally.

"It placed me in something of a quandary," sighed Mary. "Father had instructed me not to leave Kenninghall without his express permission, while the King has commanded my presence at Richmond. Richmond, as you know, has strong associations for His Majesty with his late lamented son – my husband. Faced with such a predicament, I had no real choice: His Majesty's command must be obeyed at any cost."

"Why did not you tell me of the matter earlier?" demanded her brother. "Why did not you seek my advice?"

"Dear Tom!" Mary said, softly. "I am very fond of you, my brother, and it seemed to me you had problems enough of your own. I decided not to trouble you with my concerns."

"But surely ..."

"His Majesty expressed his desire for my presence at

Richmond in the warmest terms," went on Mary, ignoring
her brother's attempt to remonstrate. "I am his daughter-in-
law after all – in truth, I suspect that the old lecher fancies me
himself!"

"Fie, sister! You speak of our noble monarch in parlance
unbefitting a lady!"

Mary shrugged. "Then I am no lady, my brother. Anyway,
the matter is settled. When one's monarch calls, one must
obey – I have ofttimes heard our lord father express himself
thus!"

"You expect to be back within a week, you say? I will tell
father that when he returns. Should your sojourn at Richmond
be prolonged, do not be surprised if father finds some means of
having you brought back forthwith to Kenninghall!"

"Criminy! I have just realised!" exclaimed Mary, in
pretended alarm. "With father and myself from home, you
and your bride-to-be will be alone in this great house. Lady
Catherine will be unchaperoned, alas!"

"We shall be alone, as you say." Lord Thomas's expression
was sardonic. "Alone, save for upwards of two hundred
servants – not to mention Bess Holland!"

"Servants are not chaperons," retorted Mary. "Servants are
not persons in the sense that you and I are persons – they care
naught for the goings-on of the nobility! They gossip and
fabricate behind our backs – but who takes notice of the
maunderings of servants? As for Bess Holland – you are surely
not suggesting, brother, that she is a fit person to be the
guardian of a maiden's honour."

"You seem on friendly enough terms with her," pointed out
Lord Thomas.

"Bess amuses me, that is all," said Mary hastily. "She is
down to earth, calls a spade a spade, and is a mine of
information about all that goes on in this household."

"With regard to the latter, that is as it should be, my sister.
She is officially the housekeeper here at Kenninghall."

"Oh, I was not referring to Bess's official duties," explained
Mary. "Those concern me not. 'Tis her knowledge of
unofficial matters that interests me. You would be surprised –

even shocked perchance – if you knew what goes on under this very roof. You would be astonished at some of the things Bess has told me."

"Things like how much she hates our lord father?" asked Lord Thomas quietly.

"How much she hates father?" asked Mary, as if he had taken leave of his wits. "You were speaking with irony no doubt!"

"Bess Holland hates our lord father," Lord Thomas said unequivocally.

"What a curious idea!" exclaimed Mary. "She has been father's mistress for twenty-seven years. She dotes on him. You are surely wrong, brother."

"She dotes on his wealth, and on the power she has achieved in this household," Lord Thomas told her. "But one day, alas, father will discover her true feelings for him."

"I feel sure you are mistaken, my brother." Mary spoke with a nonchalance she was far from feeling. "Anyway, if you remember, it was Lady Catherine we were talking about – not Bess Holland. You treat each other like strangers."

"We are strangers," said Lord Thomas. "I had hoped we would come to know each other better as the days passed, but she seems to avoid me whenever she can. She is very pretty, like a fairy-tale princess, but it seems to me she lacks warmth. I fear she has no great liking for me."

"Nay, 'tis not that, my brother."

"Have you some other explanation then?"

"Sit down here by the fireside, Tom, and I shall try to explain what is amiss. Perchance if I give you a hint, no more, as to the reason for her coldness, you will find some means of remedying the matter."

"Pray tell me what is amiss, my sister," Lord Thomas said, seating himself opposite her.

"'Tis not that she dislikes you, Tom. Be assured of that. 'Tis just that –" Mary paused tantalisingly. "Well, she is just not happy here."

"What mean you?" demanded Lord Thomas.

"I can say no more," Mary told him. "Catherine spoke to

me in confidence, and far be it from me to betray such a
secret."

"Fiddlesticks!" exclaimed her brother.

"It would be wrong for me to betray Catherine's
confidence," Mary said piously.

"Wrong, you say?" Lord Thomas smiled ruefully.
"Perchance it is. But that would not deter you, Mary of
Richmond, if it suited your purpose to speak. Lady Catherine
is my bride-to-be, and it seems to me I have a right to know if
aught is troubling her. Think you I have not noticed her
unhappiness?"

"Who could be happy here?" asked Mary. "I most
certainly am not."

"I could be happy here – with her," Lord Thomas said
quietly.

Mary looked at him quizzically. So my enigmatic brother
has conceived a regard for the virtuous Lady Catherine! she
thought.

"Oh well, in that case I suppose you have a right to know,"
she sighed. "If I do not tell you, doubtless you will find out
sooner or later. An unwilling bride finds it difficult to disguise
her unwillingness – so I am told!"

"Keep me not in suspense, sister. Tell me what you know –
or could it be that this is another of your cat-and-mouse
games?"

"Lady Catherine is in love with a certain young gentleman
who lives in one of the villages not far from Sackville Hall,"
Mary said, repeating almost word for word the tale she had
told Catherine of Lord Thomas himself. "He is a son of the
village squire and Lady Catherine had hopes of marrying him.
But her lord father refused to hearken to her pleas. He
reminded her that she was contracted to you. She protested.
Of course she protested – and who could blame her? But it
was all to no avail."

Lord Thomas looked crestfallen. "I had no idea," he said.

"Heart-broken, Lady Catherine bade farewell to the man
she loved –" Mary was enjoying herself, and the effect she was
creating, "– and, distressed and forlorn, made her departure

from Sackville. Ofttimes I have found her in her chamber weeping – and on one occasion, when she seemed more than usually distressed, she told me the whole story. I suppose she had to unburden herself to someone!"

"And that someone had to be you, my heartless sister!" said Lord Thomas. "I am glad none the less you have told me of the matter. At least I have a better understanding of the situation and can act accordingly. I shall talk to Lady Catherine, and will myself release her from the contract if she so wishes it."

"'Tis too late, my brother," Mary said sorrowfully. "The young man's father, acting on Lord Dorset's request, married him off to some local wench just one week before Lady Catherine's departure. Your bride is determined to go through with the marriage."

"You make it sound like an execution," Lord Thomas said grimly. "Ah well! I must give some thought to the matter. I want no unwilling bride. I had hoped …"

"You had hoped what?" asked Mary curiously as her brother hesitated.

He shrugged. "'Tis of no importance."

"As you say, 'tis of no importance," said Mary, concealing her disappointment at his careless acceptance of her tale. "I am glad you are taking it so philosophically. An arranged match is a mere matter of politics after all – one cannot expect *happiness*."

"Our brother's marriage was an arranged match, and yet he and Frances are idyllically happy," Lord Thomas pointed out.

"It appears so," admitted Mary grudgingly, "but that could be because Henry is away from home so much. Besides, Frances is a gentle, foolish creature with little spirit!"

"Frances is gentle and warm and loving – just the wife for one of Henry's temperament. She gives him the stability he lacks – the stability we all lack, thanks to our parents' marital battles that cast a blight on our growing-up years."

"That is quite a speech, coming from you, my enigmatic brother," Mary said tauntingly.

"Despite his flamboyance, his courage and seeming self-confidence, Henry of Surrey is basically insecure," Lord Thomas said evenly, "While you, my sister, have the hallmark of an embittered spinster."

"How dare you speak so!" exclaimed Mary furiously. "How dare you! I thought you were different from father and Henry, but I see now ..."

"I was but speaking the truth," interposed Lord Thomas mildly.

"Then if I am, as you say, an embittered spinster, what are you, my brother – tell me that!" flared Mary.

"I know not what I am, and that is the truth. I had hoped to find love and happiness in marriage as Henry has. But now, after what you have told me ..." He shrugged, and for one brief moment Mary regretted her lies. "– I know not."

Ten

Five weeks had passed since Catherine's arrival at Kenninghall, and her loneliness and homesickness had but increased with the passing of time.

The Duke treated her always with geniality and kindness, talking to her in an avuncular fashion and frequently making her laugh, but he was much away from home.

Lord Thomas seemed as much a stranger to her as ever. Invariably courteous and considerate, he nevertheless maintained an air of remoteness and Catherine suspected more than once that he was deliberately avoiding her.

She had mixed feelings about Mary. An entertaining companion at times, Mary was moody and unpredictable, and could change in an instant from smiling good-humour to a bout of ill-temper during which Catherine would find herself at the mercy of Mary's sharp tongue.

Despite her reservations about Mary, Catherine felt more bereft than ever after her departure. She sat miserably in her chamber, wondering how she would pass the time until Mary's return.

The November afternoon was unusually bright and sunny and, with sudden resolution, Catherine summoned Lucy and bade her fetch her cloak.

"I am going to take a walk in the gardens," she said. "Perhaps some fresh air will help to raise my spirits."

"There are still a few roses in the rose garden," Lucy told her. "'Tis sheltered there, so you'd not take a chill, my lady, if you sat there for a few minutes."

"Indeed I might do that, Lucy."

A few minutes later, warmly wrapped against the cold by a cloak of blue velvet, its edges and hood trimmed with broad bands of black fur that framed her face and contrasted becomingly with her fair hair, Catherine was making her way towards the gardens.

She entered the rose garden and wandered round slowly, enjoying the fresh air and the sight of the remaining roses, those hardy reminders of a summer that had gone.

A summer that had gone? Reminded of the past summer and the memories it evoked of her home and lost happiness, tears filled Catherine's eyes and she sat down forlornly on a long stone seat that overlooked the lily pond.

The beauties of nature had, after all, served merely to emphasise the contrast between their lightness and gaiety and her own dark misery.

How can I marry Lord Thomas, knowing what I know? she asked herself. He loves another, and must be as unhappy about the match as I. In truth, if it were not for the information Mary imparted to me, I believe I might conceive a regard for him. He says little, but he is handsome and his eyes are quite beautiful, and when he does speak to me his voice is warm and pleasing. Mary says he has inherited his dark brown eyes from his Plantagenet ancestors, as have the Duke and the Earl his brother. But Mary says it scornfully, as if she disapproves, while I – though I would admit it to none but myself – find his eyes curiously exciting.

I suspect that he avoids me whenever possible. He is kind and courteous whenever we meet, but 'tis clear his mind is on his lost love. What am I to do? What can I do? Hundreds of miles separate me from my home and family, and for five whole weeks I have lived among strangers.

Sometimes I wish Mary had not told me her brother's secret. Perchance if I had not known, I would still have had hope for the future. As it is, the weeks I have spent here among strangers are but a prelude to a lifetime lived in like manner ...

Overwhelmed by unhappiness, Catherine fell into a sudden fit of weeping. Realizing she was unobserved and that there was no one to bear witness to her misery, tears streamed down her cheeks unchecked. She fumbled unseeingly for her handkerchief and, drawing it from the concealed pocket of her cloak, dabbed ineffectually at her tear-stained face.

The voice near at hand made her jump.

"Dear me! Dear, dear me! Whatever is wrong, my lady?" asked the voice.

Looking up in alarm, Catherine saw through her tears the tall figure of Thomas Howard standing only a few feet away from her.

"Wrong?" she asked tremulously. "Why should you think there is aught wrong, my lord?"

He smiled then, and his smile was warm and gentle – not mocking, as Mary's would have been.

"I know not," he said, "unless it be second sight! After all, only a nincompoop would suspect there was something amiss if he came across a maiden seated alone amidst a veritable torrent of tears!"

He drew a large, lace-edged handkerchief from the pocket of his jerkin, unfolded it and handed it to her.

"Pray take my pocket handkin, my lady," he said with a bow. "'Twill serve you better than that damp cobweb you are holding at the moment."

Catherine smiled through her tears.

"Pocket handkin? I have never heard them called that before," she said.

"That is because you are not a Howard – yet. Once you are a Howard, you also will call them pocket handkins. My lady mother referred to them thus when we were tiny children, and my brother and I – and even my sister when she is in a pocket handkin mood – still do so. May I sit down here beside you for a few moments, my lady?"

"Of course, my lord," nodded Catherine, trying to repair the ravages to her face and conscious of her red-rimmed eyes. "Pray forgive my woebegone appearance."

"Woebegone! A lovely word that, is it not?" Lord Thomas smiled. "Woe be gone! One must say it as if one were casting a spell, and then, lo and behold, one feels better at once. You do feel better, do you not?"

She nodded, not trusting herself to speak. "I feel better now that you are here, my lord. You nearly made me laugh!"

"Peter's bones! What an accusation! Thomas Howard nearly made his bride-to-be laugh – whatever next!"

She laughed softly. "Why did you come here?" she asked shyly.

"To talk to you."

"But how did you know I was here?"

"I saw you leave the house, from an upstairs window."

"How could that be, my lord?" asked Catherine mischievously. "I did not leave from an upstairs window."

"You are better," said Lord Thomas smilingly. "You certainly are better. Carry on like that and you will be one of the pocket handkin brigade before you know it."

"Forgive me, my lord," Catherine said contritely, but unable to repress a smile. "You were explaining about how you came to be here."

"I was looking out of an upstairs window, when I saw you leave the house," he said gravely. "It suddenly occurred to me that at last we had a chance to be together, to really get to know each other without interruption."

"I thought you did not wish to get to know me," Catherine said in a small voice. "I thought you were avoiding me."

"And I thought you were avoiding me," Lord Thomas said gently. "Now I am not so sure."

"Pray tell me why you have changed your mind, my lord."

"'Twas something my brother told me – and which my sister unwittingly corroborated yesterday."

"What did Lady Mary tell you – or is it a secret?"

"According to my sister, it was a secret – she, alas, finds it difficult to keep a secret."

"What was this secret, my lord?"

"First, my lady, permit me to ask you a question or two."

"Of course, my lord."

"Did my sister tell you of my lady love?"

Catherine looked startled but then, lowering her gaze to hide her misery, seemed lost for words.

"Did she tell you that I had a deep regard for a certain

maiden in one of the neighbouring villages?'' persisted Lord Thomas.

Catherine nodded, but remained silent.

"Then no doubt she also told you I had been forced to relinquish the maiden of my heart because of our marriage contract. Is it not so?''

"She said something of the sort,'' admitted Catherine.

"And you believed her?''

"Of course, my lord.''

"Would you still believe her if I told you that she told me a similar story?''

"A similar story? Why would she do that, my lord?''

"Perchance we should leave that question for the moment,'' said Lord Thomas. "First, I would like to tell you that similar story.''

"Pray continue, my lord.''

"I will repeat my sister's story verbatim in so far as I am able: 'Lady Catherine is in love with a certain young gentleman who lives in one of the villages not far from Sackville Hall,' she said. 'He is a son of the village squire and Lady Catherine had hopes of marrying him. But her lord father refused to hearken to her pleas. He reminded her that she was contracted to you. She protested. Of course she protested – and who could blame her? But it was all to no avail.' ''

Catherine gazed at him in wide-eyed astonishment.

"Lady Mary said that – about me?'' she asked incredulously.

"She did indeed,'' Lord Thomas said evenly.

"And you believed her?'' she asked, just as he had done.

"I made pretence of believing her – one must play my sister at her own game,'' Lord Thomas said, his eyes twinkling. "My sister is bored and frustrated, and takes pleasure from making mischief and trying to make others as unhappy as she is herself. My brother got wind of what was afoot and gave me fair warning, so Mary's fabrication came as no surprise to me.''

"Then you did not believe her, my lord?''

"Why else am I here today?" he asked. "Mary's inventions had the reverse effect from that intended. Instead of building a wall between us, she opened my eyes to the truth."

"And what is the truth, my lord?"

Lord Thomas made pretence of not having heard the question.

"I resolved that, as soon as Mary and her mischief-making were out of the way, I would seek for an opportunity of talking to you alone," he said. "I saw my opportunity this afternoon – here we are isolated from Bess Holland and her minions!"

"I am so glad, my lord," Catherine said softly.

"Glad that I came to talk to you – or that my sister's story was false?" Lord Thomas asked, smilingly.

"Both."

"And now that you know I was heart-free when you came here, pray tell me the truth, my lady. Is the thought of marrying me anathema to you?"

Faced with such a direct question, Catherine hesitated.

"My lord, you say that you were heart-free," she said. "Is one to assume therefore that you are heart-free no longer?"

"You have the makings of a diplomat, my lady," smiled Lord Thomas. "You parry one question by asking another. However, to answer your question – you may indeed assume that I am heart-free no longer. And now that I have answered your question, pray do me the honour of answering mine."

Catherine's dismay at his answer was ill-concealed.

"But since you are heart-free no longer ..."

"Pray answer me, my lady," he said sternly. "And, lest you have mislaid the question, I will repeat it: Is the thought of marrying me anathema to you?"

"We are already married – in law," she said evasively.

"Our marriage was lawfully contracted thirteen years ago, but we shall not be truly man and wife till after the Nuptial Mass and the bedding," he said plainly.

Catherine blushed but said nothing, refusing to meet his gaze.

"Again I ask you – for I must know the truth, however unacceptable it may be – whether the thought of becoming my bride, in the full sense, is unpleasing to you." Lord Thomas's voice was quiet but insistent.

"I am not yet sure of my feelings, my lord," Catherine said, "I have been lonely and homesick since my arrival here at Kenninghall. Perchance had you been here to welcome me upon my arrival ..."

She fell silent, confused by her own feelings. Is that the truth? she thought. Am I not yet sure of my feelings? Ever since our first meeting, I have always been aware of Lord Thomas, conscious of his presence, and I was hurt by his apparent lack of interest in me. Today, I have seen a side of him I have never seen before. He sought me out, wishing to speak to me alone, and has shown me patience and sympathy, it is clear he has some concern for my feelings.

"That I was not here to greet you on your arrival was indeed unfortunate," he was saying. "Believe me, my lady, no one regrets it as much as I do. Perchance if I were to offer you an explanation, it would help in some measure to mitigate your understandable sense of grievance."

"His Grace has already explained the reason for your absence," Catherine told him.

"My lord father and I do not always see matters from the same angle," explained Lord Thomas. "Thus his explanation and mine might differ in some aspects. I feel just as certain that I can trust you to keep the explanation to yourself, as I am certain that I could not trust my sister in like case."

"I should speak of it to no one, my lord."

"When, a few months ago, my brother, Henry of Surrey, was relieved of his command of the English forces in France, he returned to England under something of a cloud," explained Lord Thomas. "Because of his lifelong friendship with the King's illegitimate son, the Duke of Richmond, Henry had always been greatly favoured by His Majesty, but he returned to Court to discover that, his enemies having worked unceasingly to discredit him in his absence, His Majesty's affection for him seemed to have waned."

"I have always heard it said that His Majesty will hear no ill of the Earl of Surrey," said Catherine.

"That was indeed the case – until recently," Lord Thomas told her. "My brother, true to form, lost no time after his return in publicly accusing the Seymours of conspiring in his absence to discredit him with the King. In so doing he merely increased the King's wrath. My lord father, fearing where Henry's reckless fury would lead him, decided he must journey to London in order to warn him against acting rashly. He wished me to accompany him for, curiously enough, there are times when I seem better able than my lord father to make Henry see sense."

"You are different in temperament, and yet there is a close bond between you," said Catherine. "I have noticed that, my lord, and Lady Frances corroborated it. She greatly values your influence on my lord of Surrey."

"I suppose one might call me a sobering influence," Lord Thomas said with a wry smile. "I fear that my brother outshines me in most things – but that in no way weakens the bond between us."

"I gather that your efforts on your brother's behalf were not in vain, my lord," said Catherine.

"He did give heed to our warning, God be praised, despite his fury at the way he had been received at Court," Lord Thomas told her. "His Majesty certainly showed Henry a coolness that was a poor return for his skilful leadership of the French campaign, but he chose to ignore the accusations of treachery and banished Henry to Mount Surrey. Henry would have remonstrated with His Majesty at this, but we managed to persuade him that it was politic to lie fallow for a few months in Norfolk. Thus Henry returned with my lord father and myself just two days after your arrival, my lady."

"Thank you for telling me of this, my lord," said Catherine. "I see now that you had no choice."

"His Majesty will doubtless reinstate Henry in his affections – if Henry plays his cards carefully," said Lord Thomas. "But my brother's pride and his refusal to compromise can be dangerous, and could have serious consequences for him – and for my lord father."

"And for you, my lord?" Catherine asked, and he registered

her note of concern.

"I keep a low profile in so far as I am permitted to," he told her. "Court life holds little appeal for me but, as my father's son, it is incumbent upon me to take my rightful place at all royal functions. My lord father is the greatest soldier of our time – even his enemies would not deny that – and has passed on much of his military skill to Henry. Whilst at times I must follow where they lead, I am happiest when here in East Anglia, administering my lord's Norfolk and Suffolk estates during his frequent absences. I fear I am really a dull fellow!"

"I do not see you as dull," Catherine said shyly. "You are handsome and kind, and you make me smile when I am sad and ..."

Catherine paused, hesitant of expressing herself further.

"And you do not regard marriage to me as too dreadful a calamity?" Lord Thomas interposed with a smile. "Could that be what you were about to say?"

"Perchance when we know each other a little better ..."

"I trust we shall shortly know each other a great deal better, my lady," put in Lord Thomas. "Our wedding day is a mere two months away. We shall be married on 20th January in Westminster Abbey, as befits the son and daughter of two noble houses."

"I have never been to London, my lord," Catherine told him. "The thought of being stared at by so many strangers makes me feel quite nervous!"

"Remember that I shall be there beside you, and I will no longer be a stranger. I suspect that already I am less of a stranger than I was an hour ago. Is it not so, my lady?"

Catherine smiled shyly and nodded her agreement.

"Then let us meet here again at the same time upon the morrow," suggested Lord Thomas, "and each day following until that of our bridal. Thus with each passing day we shall feel less like strangers."

"What if it should be raining, my lord?"

"By my faith, you ask the most astonishing questions!" exclaimed Lord Thomas banteringly. "What if the roof should fall in? What if there is an earthquake and Kenninghall is swallowed into the ground? What if I should fall from my horse and break my neck?''

"Pray do not speak of such a dreadful happening!" shuddered Catherine. "I think I could not bear it if anything like that happened to you!"

"Why do you say that, my lady?"

"But for you, I should be quite alone here at Kenninghall, my lord."

"But for me, you would not be here at Kenninghall at all," he pointed out. "In truth then, 'tis I who am to blame for your unhappiness – think well on that, my lady."

"My unhappiness?" Catherine's question seemed to be addressed to herself rather than to Lord Thomas.

"Should some disaster befall me, you would be sent back to Sackville forthwith," persisted Lord Thomas. "Then, in a very short while, your lord father would be negotiating another match for you – one, God willing, that would be more to your liking."

"I have no desire for another match, my lord," Catherine said firmly.

"You wish to enter a convent perchance, and spend your life in prayer and contemplation?"

"Nay, my lord, the religious life holds no appeal for me."

"Marriage or a convent – there is no other choice for a lady of nobility," pointed out Lord Thomas. "I feel sure you are aware of that."

"You misunderstand me, my lord," Catherine said slowly and looking ahead of her as if she feared to meet his gaze. "When I said I have no desire for another match, I meant – I meant... "

"What did you mean, my lady," prompted Lord Thomas.

"I meant that marriage with you, my lord, has much to recommend it," Catherine said primly.

"Such an ambiguous statement needs qualifying, my lady," said Lord Thomas. "Was it prompted by duty to your lord father – or could it be there is hope that you will yet conceive a regard for me?"

Catherine hesitated, confused by her sudden change of

heart and seeking for the right words with which to answer.

"My lord, pray ask me that question again upon the morrow," she said at length. "By then, I should be better able to express myself."

"It shall be as you wish, my lady," agreed Lord Thomas, getting to his feet. "Permit me to accompany you back to the house now – there is a deepening chill in the air. I will meet you here again upon the morrow. Meanwhile, I shall give no hint to anyone of today's meeting, but shall cherish the hope that in a very little while all will be well between us."

Eleven

The Earl of Surrey and Lady Frances dined at Kenninghall that evening. At the end of the meal, Catherine, who had a great liking for Frances, withdrew with her to the solar, where Surrey and Lord Thomas would later rejoin them.

"Catherine, I can contain my curiosity no longer," said Frances as soon as they were seated. "What has happened to you since last we met?"

"Happened?" asked Catherine in surprise. "'Tis a mere seven days since I saw you last. What could have happened?"

"That is what I am asking you," smiled Frances. "Could it be that Mary's absence is the reason for your joy?"

"My joy?"

"Catherine, my dear, pray do not take it amiss when I tell you that, each time I have seen you ere now, I have been aware of your unhappiness," Frances said earnestly. "You looked like a little lost child, and I would like to have kept you at Mount Surrey and cosseted you as if you were one of my own brood."

"Dear Frances!" Catherine said, touched by her gentle concern.

"I mentioned it to my lord, but he laughed and teased me, and said that if four children as well as the one I am carrying are not enough to occupy me, then we should offer a novena to Our Lady, asking that our next be quadruplets," Frances said lightly. "I am delighted to see such a change in you. Since you were apparently unaware of it, the explanation must lie in Mary's absence. Poor Mary! She too is an unhappy person – but she, alas, is her own worst enemy!"

"If I give the appearance of being happy, then I suppose it must be due to Mary's absence – indirectly," Catherine said thoughtfully. "You are right of course, Frances. I am much happier than I was – though, curious to relate, I had not realized it till you drew my attention to it. How foolish that must sound!"

"Nay, 'tis not foolishness. 'Tis a quirk of human nature that we accept happiness as our right – 'tis only when we are unhappy that we learn, through its loss, to recognize happiness. You say that this change in you has come about as an *indirect* result of Mary's absence. How so?"

"Frances, greatly as I appreciate and value your concern for me, I cannot answer your question as yet," Catherine told her. "We agreed not to speak of it, Lord Thomas and I."

For a few moments, Frances gazed at her in disconcerting silence. Then she smiled.

"I see," she said slowly. "Thank you for telling me, Catherine."

"But I have told you nothing. I have… "

"You have told me everything – unknowingly!" insisted Frances. "Your eyes lit up just then as you spoke the name of your betrothed in a way that could mean one thing only – you are in love with him, God be praised!"

"I fail to see how… "

"Mary did her best to cause a misunderstanding between you," went on Frances. "I realized that and spoke to my lord of the matter, and he talked to his brother and warned him to be on his guard. So Mary's plan to keep you apart was thwarted, thanks be to God, and all is now well. You and your betrothed have fallen into each other's arms – metaphorically speaking of course! Oh, Catherine, I am so happy for you!"

"But it is not like that at all," protested Catherine. "Mary did cause mischief – you are right there – but in truth I was more despondent than ever after her departure. Beset by misery and boredom I decided to take a walk in the garden this afternoon, imagining that the fresh air would enliven my spirits. Lord Thomas found me sitting weeping in the rose-garden. He was kind and understanding, and then we talked for a while and – well, that is all!"

"When are you meeting him again – in the rose-garden?" Frances asked, innocently.

"How do you know I am?"

"I just know – that is all," shrugged Frances. "My lord maintains that I develop a sixth sense whenever I am with child, so please forgive me, dear Catherine, if I seem too perceptive for comfort!"

"Oh, Frances, I could forgive you anything!" exclaimed Catherine impulsively. "No wonder your lord loves you so devotedly! Your marriage is spoken of with awe by many, I understand."

"You speak as if a happy marriage is some sort of phenomenon," smiled Frances. "I feel sure that you too will have a happy marriage."

"Mary would laugh you to scorn for speaking thus! Whilst marriages between strangers are the norm and people marry only for political advantage and the continuance of their line, happy marriages must surely remain a rarity. You and your lord are truly fortunate – and yet you seem to take your good fortune for granted."

"Nay, you are wrong there, Catherine." Frances was suddenly serious. "Never for one moment do I take my good fortune for granted. It is not always wise to love as I love my lord. What if one should lose the subject of one's devotion? The measure of one's love would then become the measure of one's grief – to love too greatly is to live with fear."

"Frances, you are suddenly sorrowful," said Catherine. "Forgive me – I did not mean to cause you pain by my words. You speak as if you fear for the future… "

"We were talking of you, if you remember," interposed Frances. "My lord and his brother will be joining us soon, so I beg you satisfy my curiosity."

"But I know not… "

"Pray remember, Catherine, that if I seem to be prying, it is solely out of a wish to see you and my brother-in-law happily married," put in Frances. "I hold him in great affection, as does my lord husband."

"I am to meet him in the rose-garden again on the morrow," Catherine told her then. "I was upset and confused when we met this afternoon, and needed time to think and discover my true feelings."

"And?"

"After I returned to the house, I sat for two whole hours thinking about my meeting with Lord Thomas. Then suddenly I recognized the truth – that all my thoughts and hopes were concentrated on tomorrow's meeting, on our being together again and on what I would say to him."

"So it is as I thought," said Frances delightedly. "You are in love with him. Oh Catherine, dear Catherine – I am so happy for you, so very happy! I can scarcely wait to tell my lord."

"I did not say I was in – in love with him, as you put it."

"You do not need to. Maybe you are as yet unaware of the fact, but it makes no difference," insisted Frances. "You *are* in love with your betrothed. God be praised, 'twill be a love match after all – my prayers have been answered!"

"You speak with some confidence, Frances, but supposing you were right about my feelings for my betrothed – just supposing, mind! – what makes you think my feelings are reciprocated?"

"That sixth sense of mine, I suppose," smiled Frances.

"Believe me, I know nothing of Lord Thomas's regard for me," pointed out Catherine. "He is courteous and kind, and seems now to be less like a stranger, but… "

"But you have yet to discover his feelings for you," Frances finished for her, as she heard footsteps coming along the passageway towards the solar. "Tomorrow then, dear Catherine, will be a meeting of discovery. I shall await the outcome with confidence. Now, I must stop grinning like a Cheshire cat, and compose myself. Otherwise, the very instant my lord sets eyes on me, he will know I have something up my sleeve and could well ask awkward questions."

Twelve

As if the November weather was on their side and wished to bestow a blessing on their meeting, the afternoon that followed was filled with a pale winter sunlight that lent colour to the few remaining roses in the garden.

Catherine reached the rose-garden at the time arranged, to find Lord Thomas already there.

His back to her, he was gazing down at the lily pond, unaware of her arrival. Catherine paused in the stone archway that gave entrance to that section of the garden and watched him for a few moments. She had not seen him since the previous evening, having remained in her chamber all the morning.

He was wearing neither gown nor cloak, but was clad in doublet and hose of crimson velvet, the doublet being worn over a white shirt exquisitely embroidered and frilled at the wrists. His sleeveless, V-shaped jerkin, open to the waist to disclose much of the doublet, was also of crimson velvet. His only jewellery was a heavy gold chain and medallion, and the gold signet ring he used for sealing letters.

Even as Catherine watched, a sudden light breeze ruffled his dark hair, giving him an appealing boyishness.

He looks, thought Catherine, surprisingly vulnerable, as if he feels as lonely and defenceless as I. Alas, I am being foolish!

He caught sight of her then, and strode forward to greet her, his sudden smile leaving her in no doubt of his pleasure at her arrival.

"I feared that, after all, you would not come here today," he said, taking her hand and drawing her gently towards the stone seat. "'Tis good to see you, my lady."

"Why did you fear I would not come?" she asked.

"Our meeting yesterday gave me hope of future joy and happiness," he told her. "I feared to put the matter to the test, lest I discovered I was mistaken in thinking that you no longer viewed me with mistrust."

"At no time did I view you with mistrust, my lord," Catherine assured him. "Always you have shown me kindness and courtesy. But you seemed also to display a certain coldness towards me, as if I was in some way unpleasing to you."

"And that is why you readily accepted my sister's story?"

"I suppose it is," she nodded. "'Twas foolish of me, and very naïve, to be so easily taken in, but your sister's story offered an explanation for your seeming coldness towards me."

Lord Thomas was silent for a few moments as if he were weighing his words carefully before he spoke.

"My lady, you leave me no other choice than to be completely honest with you," he said solemnly then.

"Honest? Then you have some dark secret after all?" He heard the note of alarm in her voice.

"I trust that when you have heard what I have to say, my lady, you will know me a little better, and as a consequence be able to judge your own feelings the better," he said quietly.

I already know my own feelings, Catherine thought. Did not I remain awake most of last night, pondering on our meeting yesterday and on what my lord had said? Did not I think also of Frances's words, of her conviction that already I had formed a strong regard for him? I fell asleep at last, only to have strange dreams and disturbing fantasies: I heard Mary's voice re-telling her lies, and saw Frances's smile vanish to be replaced by tears. My lord and I seemed to have become separated, for I held out my arms beseechingly to him, but he was a long way off. I cried out to him in my sleep and tried to reach him and draw him closer but, even as I did so, he moved further away from me. I awoke with tears on my cheeks, and a new knowledge …

"Pray continue, my lord," she said.

"I loved you from the very first moment I saw you," he said

simply. "I had longed for our first meeting, whilst also dreading it. Like Henry and Mary, I too had suffered from the insecurity of our childhood, and I knew that nothing save a love match would be acceptable to me."

"Was your childhood as insecure as is said?" Catherine asked, touched by his words but unwilling as yet to commit herself.

He nodded. "Our parents were constantly at loggerheads, and our lady mother was not of a maternal temperament."

"But your lord father was ofttimes away from home, I understand – much as your brother is nowadays," said Catherine.

"He was indeed. He was frequently engaged on some military campaign, leading His Majesty's armies into France, Scotland and the Border country."

"Then since your parents were so often apart, why did their incompatibility affect you so deeply, my lord?" asked Catherine, her own happy memories of childhood making it hard to understand. "You were brought up in luxury, with an army of servants to answer your every need. And you had each other."

"When my lord father came home, at once the violent quarrels and the bickering started up again, and the situation became even worse after Mary was born and Bess Holland became my father's mistress," Lord Thomas explained. "Father permitted Bess to usurp my mother's position in the household, and ordered my mother to remain in her own apartments."

"Your mother could surely have refused."

"Oh, she did! She did, indeed," said Lord Thomas grimly. "But to no avail. Mother was not one to give in without a fight. She stormed and raged and, after one particularly violent scene, was locked in her chamber and Bess was given possession of the keys. Eventually, my mother sought audience with the King and begged him to intercede for her, on the grounds that she, a direct descendant of Edward III, had been forced to take second place to a serving-woman. His Majesty, having need I suppose of my father's goodwill, dismissed her plea, and my mother never returned to Kenninghall, preferring to live in comparatively humble circumstances elsewhere."

"'Tis difficult to imagine your lord father treating his wife, the mother of his children, in such a manner," remarked Catherine. "He seems to me to be a kindly gentleman."

"So he is – to those who share his views and give deference to his high lineage," Lord Thomas told her. "He is a generous master and overlord – his servants and the peasantry of Norfolk and Suffolk hold him in affection – but he is also a formidable enemy."

"But the Duchess is his wife."

"Methinks one cannot make fair judgements of other people's marriages," Lord Thomas said slowly. "There is much of which one is ignorant, and both parties make their own case good. If you knew my mother, perchance you would better understand why she is not an easy person to love. Every man, it seems to me, needs a woman's love, and love begets love – had my mother given my father love and happiness, perchance he would not have become involved with Bess Holland."

"Men ofttimes take a mistress – so I understand," Catherine said diffidently. "Why then did your lord father not do so – but with discretion?"

"My father is a law unto himself," Lord Thomas told her. "He does in truth regard his lineage as higher than that of the King – though to declare such publicly would be tantamount to signing his own death warrant! Just as, in the North, the saying is: 'There is no king but Percy!' in East Anglia the saying is: 'There is no king but Tom of Norfolk!'"

"Would not it have been better for you children if your mother had taken you with her and set up a separate establishment elsewhere, my lord?" asked Catherine.

"Father would not have permitted it," was the reply. "And, in truth, I am not sure if mother wished to take Henry and Mary – I was her favourite you see!"

"Why so?"

"She disliked Henry, declaring he was father over again, and seemed to think of Mary's birth as synonymous with the arrival of Bess Holland," explained Lord Thomas. "She dotes on me and would have taken me with her had father agreed. I was inconsolable after her departure and, whilst Henry and I were always good friends, I always felt deprived of care and affection."

"Did your father not show you affection?"

"He favoured Henry – like my mother, he saw Henry as a reflection of himself – though he treated me always with kindness. Bess Holland disliked me – perchance because I was my mother's favourite! I became quiet and introverted, preferring the company of local farmers to that of the nobility; and, when the time came for taking my place as my father's second son, I attended Court only when expediency, duty, and my noble lineage demanded it."

"Alas, that your upbringing was so different from mine!" sighed Catherine. "Mine was such a happy childhood, full of love and affection and gaiety."

"Always I nurtured a hope that when you, to whom I had been contracted in boyhood, became truly my bride, my loneliness would be at an end," Lord Thomas told her. "I built on that hope as the years went by, imagining how you would look, how you would speak, how you would be dressed – latterly, I had pictured us as being as idyllically happy as Henry and Frances."

"And when at last you met me, you were disappointed," Catherine said sadly. "I failed to live up to your expectations. That then is why you seemed so cold and distant towards me."

"You are so wrong, my lady," he said. "So very wrong! Always I had pictured my dream bride with pale blonde hair like that of a fairy-tale princess – I know not why, though it is said that opposites attract! – and with eyes as green as emeralds."

He hesitated then, as if he were choosing his next words with care.

"And?" prompted Catherine softly. "There is an 'and,' is there not, my lord?"

"My dream bride wore a green gown that enhanced the

colour of her eyes," he said. "My lady Greensleeves, I called her."

For a few moments there was silence between them and then Lord Thomas got up and stood looking down at her.

"On that day I first saw you, I knew you were the bride of my dreams," he said, his voice deep with emotion. "You were the epitome of all my hopes. You were wearing a green gown, the gown I had seen in my dreams – in that first moment I saw you, my dream had become reality. You were indeed my lady Greensleeves."

"Then it was surprise I saw on your face – not disappointment," Catherine said slowly.

"It was surprise – and something more," he told her. "I could not believe the evidence of my eyes. I imagined that Fortune was playing some cruel prank on me; that, though you looked to be the bride of my dreams, I would yet find some flaw in you that would prevent your becoming mine."

"And?" murmured Catherine.

"Only you can tell me whether or not you are the maiden of my dreams." He took her hands and drew her gently to her feet. "Only you, my lady, can tell me if there is hope that in time you could love me as already I love you – with a deep devotion."

Catherine's eyes were bright with tears. "My lord, you can do more than hope. I realized after our meeting yesterday that I was in love with you – and had been so since our very first meeting. Our feelings in those first moments must have been mutual – though it has taken me five whole weeks, and your sister's meddling, to recognize my regard for you. It was your seeming coldness towards me that made me so forlorn ..."

Her words trembled into silence, and at once he took her in his arms and kissed her tenderly on the lips.

"This is the happiest day of my life, beloved," he said then, his voice vibrant with emotion. "Our Lady has answered my prayers and has sent you to me as a blessing – albeit an undeserved blessing – and I swear I will do my utmost to be worthy of your love."

"Yesterday morning I realized with alarm that our wedding

day was a mere eight weeks hence," sighed Catherine.
"Today those eight weeks seem like a lifetime!"

"We shall see each other often," he said. "We will meet like
this in the garden whenever possible – each afternoon
perchance, if the weather is on our side."

"We shall meet here again on the morrow?"

He smiled and kissed her again.

"On the morrow," he assured her. "If it is raining, we will
make our way to the summer-house instead. In a few days'
time, I shall be paying a short visit to London, alas – my father
has requested my presence there – but I shall be gone for no
more than a week at the outside."

"A week?" asked Catherine in dismay. "How shall I
manage without you for a whole week, my lord? With your
lord father and Mary away also, there will be no one here but
the servants."

"I shall not be leaving until after Mary's return," he told
her.

"The thought of Mary's companionship gives me little joy,
my lord," pouted Catherine. "I would prefer, in view of her
mischief-making, to leave her severely alone."

"You could if you wish spend the week of my absence at
Mount Surrey – I have no doubt Frances would be delighted
to have your company," Lord Thomas told her, and then he
smiled wickedly. "Equally, you might prefer to remain here at
Kenninghall and use the opportunity to get even with my
sister."

"How so?"

"You could tell her that you informed me during her
absence that you knew of my romantic attachment for another
maiden, and that I had admitted it. You could further tell her
that a quarrel had ensued, and that as a result you had sent a
messenger to Sackville Hall begging your lord father to fetch
you home and have the marriage contract revoked."

Catherine smiled. "I might do just that, my lord!" she said.

"I would like to see Mary's face when you told her. She
would be forced to admit her deception then. A word of
warning though, my lady – be wary of my sister! She is

untrustworthy, as you have already discovered, but there is something else you may not have discovered."

"What is that, my lord?"

"She is on friendly terms with Bess Holland. She pours scorn on Bess Holland behind her back, and speaks of her with disdain, but in truth she is too friendly with her for comfort – even perchance for safety."

"What harm could Bess Holland do, my lord?" asked Catherine. "She is really no more than an upper servant, despite appearances to the contrary – the fact that she is your lord father's mistress does not make her any less a servant. What possible harm could she do?"

"Plenty. And that because she has been my father's mistress – and confidante – for twenty-seven years," Lord Thomas told her. "'Tis my belief she hates my father, and would not hesitate to do him a mischief if she saw her way to doing herself some good at the same time! Please God I am mistaken, but again I say to you beware of my sister and Bess Holland."

"I will, my lord, have no fear," Catherine assured him. "I shall never trust Mary again, needless to say – and I have known an instinctive mistrust of Bess Holland ever since I arrived here at Kenninghall."

"Then we need speak no more of the matter," smiled Lord Thomas.

"It is so lovely being here with you, my lord," sighed Catherine. "Pray kiss me again. I love being kissed. Indeed I think I would like to be kissed all over."

"On my faith, it would seem I am to have a wicked hussy for a bride!" he said with mock severity. "I doubt not though that I can tame her!"

"My lord, have you ever – ever ..." Catherine paused and lowered her gaze.

"Have I ever what?" asked Lord Thomas. "Pray tell me what troubles you, my lady."

"Have you ever bedded with anyone?" Her voice was small and shy.

He looked at her for a moment, as if he were choosing his words carefully before he spoke.

"I have indeed," he said at length.

"Pray tell me of it, my lord," she said in a hurt tone.

"Henry and I used to sleep in the same bed when we were children, so one could say I had bedded with him, and ..."

"You are teasing me, my lord," complained Catherine. "You knew I did not mean that. I was asking whether you had ever slept with – with a woman."

"A woman? Maidens maybe. But a woman? Let me see." He considered the matter. "None, and that is the truth – apart from Bess Holland of course!"

"Mother of God!" exclaimed Catherine, her eyes wide with horror. "You are telling me that you have slept with that – that – with your father's mistress?"

"Occasionally – and only when father was away from home."

"I am deeply shocked, my lord. You admit your sin quite glibly. Mistress Holland is twice your age and is old enough to be your mother!"

"You are right there, beloved."

"Pray do not address me in such a term, my lord. Keep such endearments for your doxies. Did you address *her* in such a manner – as your beloved?"

"I doubt it, beloved. Of course it was a long time ago, and ..."

"Spare me the details, my lord."

"You did ask, remember. And 'tis scarcely of importance, beloved ..."

"Pray do not ..."

"Henry slept with her too, beloved – it must run in the family!"

"My lord, I know not what to say. That you could have brought yourself to bed with a woman like Bess Holland!"

"Bed with her?" he asked in a shocked tone. "Bed with her? What are you suggesting, my lady? Would Thomas Howard bed with his father's whore?"

"But you said ..."

"I know perfectly well what I said, and it was certainly not that, my lady." His voice conveyed a deliberate coldness.

"The idea! In reply to your question, I told you that a long time ago my brother and I had slept with Mistress Holland. I was seven years of age and suffering an attack of measles. Whilst the fever was at its height Mistress Holland, who in our parents' absence was responsible for our well-being, sat with us throughout the night, watching over us whilst we slept."

"I see, my lord," Catherine said in a small voice, trying to avoid his gaze.

"Jesu Maria!" he exclaimed suddenly. "You surely did not imagine that I – that we – that ... Lady Catherine, I confess myself deeply shocked that you, a virtuous maiden, could even dream of such a thing!"

She looked up at him and saw that he was smiling wickedly.

"You were teasing me!" she said. "You were teasing me all the time. Fie, my lord! I should really be quite vexed with you."

"And you are not, my lady?"

"Well – " She paused tantalisingly. "Only the teeniest bit vexed!"

"I was teasing you." He was suddenly serious. "Perhaps because I saw it as a means of testing your reaction to the truth."

"Then there is something else?"

"There is something else," he nodded gravely.

"Pray tell me of it, my lord."

"Catherine, I love you with all my heart," he said, addressing her informally for the first time, "and it is my earnest desire that no dark secret should lie between us."

"Then there is a dark secret?"

"Like most young men, I have enjoyed an occasional amorous adventure," he admitted, and this time there was no doubting his sincerity. "Before my brother married and became a *comparatively* reformed character, he and I sometimes rode into Norwich for an evening's entertainment. When I was nineteen, I fell in love with a maiden, the daughter of an innkeeper, and she later bore me a boy child. Apart from the innkeeper and his daughter, none knows of this save my lord father and Henry – the innkeeper has been generously bribed by my father to keep his mouth shut and is well satisfied with the arrangement."

"And what arrangement is that, my lord?" asked Catherine uneasily.

"I maintain the child and his mother, and both are well provided for," Lord Thomas told her. "When the child is older, I shall see to it that he is suitably educated and, as is customary, I shall then acknowledge him as my bastard son."

"I see, my lord," Catherine managed to say, despite her sudden jealousy. "Thank you for telling me."

"I wished to tell you of the matter myself, lest you should later learn of it from someone else. I want no more malicious tongues wagging and causing a rift between us – had Mary known my secret, she would have made good use of it by now!"

"Then in fact, my lord, your sister's tale was not far from the truth."

"In fact it was very far from the truth," Lord Thomas insisted. "The affair with my son's mother is long past, and has no connection with marriage or your arrival here."

"Did you love her – the mother of your son?" Conscious of stabbing jealousy, Catherine could not resist the question.

"I thought I loved her – at the time," he admitted. "But it was no more than a passing infatuation, for as the months passed she ceased to interest me. She has since married and has, I understand, borne her husband several children."

"And you no longer think of her, my lord?"

"I think of her only in relation to my son."

"You love your son?"

He nodded. "Of course. Would you think better of me if I denied it?"

"You are right, my lord," Catherine admitted. "For a few moments I knew jealousy of your son, but I was being foolish. After all, you were not bound to tell me of his existence – I am grateful to you for your honesty."

"How glad I am that you know the truth, Catherine, that there are now no guilty secrets separating us." He smiled suddenly. "That is all I have to tell you of the past – there are, so far as I can recall, no more skeletons in my particular cupboard!"

Despite her words, Catherine was more disturbed by his disclosures than she would have admitted, and her voice when she spoke next was a trifle distant.

"It is time I returned to the house, my lord," she said. "Now that the sun has gone, it seems much colder."

"I will accompany you," Lord Thomas said at once. "I trust we shall meet here again upon the morrow."

"If the weather is clement –" Catherine's tone suggested that she regarded it as highly unlikely. "– I shall again take a walk in the garden. It is up to you, my lord, whether or not you choose to be here at the same time. The garden is yours – like the house and myself, to say nothing of your bastard, it is Howard property!"

"So you are angry with me," he said quietly, as they made their way towards the house. "In spite of your words, your seeming appreciation of my having told you the truth, you are greatly displeased."

"Believe that if you wish, my lord."

"I hoped to spare you pain by telling you of the matter now, instead of risking your making a discovery later that could well cast a cloud over our marriage. I trust, when you have had time to think about it, you will realize that, had I loved you less, I would have shrugged the matter aside and left you to find out for yourself."

"I bid you farewell for the time being, my lord," Catherine said carelessly. "I shall take supper in my chamber."

His voice when he spoke next was cold and uncompromising, and Catherine was beset by a conflict of emotions.

"Even for you, my lady," he said, "I will not disown my son."

They had reached the terrace by this time and Catherine paused briefly. "Pray do not trouble to accompany me further, my lord. I know the way and have a sudden desire for my own company – 'twill be good to meditate alone."

A prey to misgiving, Lord Thomas watched her enter the house. To meditate alone! he thought. My lady Catherine is hurt and upset – and I know not even now if she truly loves me. One moment she welcomes and encourages my kisses, and the next she is behaving like a nun! To meditate, indeed! I love her with all my heart and soul – please God I have not caused an irreparable rift between us by telling her the truth.

Whatever the outcome, I do not regret my disclosure. There must be no secret between us that could mar our marriage. True love must be built on honesty and trust. Ah me! I must needs contain my soul in patience till the morrow. Perchance then I shall discover where my lady's meditation has led her!

Thirteen

On her return to her chamber, Catherine removed her cloak with Lucy's assistance, and then, dismissing Lucy, seated herself for a long time by the fire.

Beset by a mixture of feelings since her encounter with Lord Thomas, she did in truth need time to think. Two days ago, Lord Thomas had been all but a stranger – a cold and distant stranger, as it had seemed to her.

Suddenly he was no longer a stranger. They had talked and had got to know each other, and Lord Thomas had declared himself in love with her. Realizing then for the first time, the strength of her own regard for him, she had been overwhelmed by unlooked-for happiness, by the knowledge that the dreaded day of her wedding was now eagerly awaited.

But then Lord Thomas had revealed his secret and again Catherine's feelings had undergone a change. Again he had seemed like a stranger.

Of course, she thought to herself as she held her hands closer to the fire to warm them, he need not have told me. He told me because he wished there to be no secrets between us, nothing that could later cast a blight upon our marriage.

He loves me, he says, with all his heart. Did he once say as much to the mother of his son? He implied that there were also others during those visits to Norwich with his brother.

But all men behave thus, it is said. Rare is the nobleman who does not have at least one bastard to support. Men brag of their conquests among themselves, seeming to regard their by-blows as proof of their maleness, and Lord Thomas, it seems, is no different. Women, I suppose, see it otherwise.

Has this knowledge I have acquired changed my newly-found regard for my betrothed? Do I no longer wish to marry him, as I did before he told me?

Perchance now that he has discovered my reaction to his news, he will think less well of me. Perchance at this very moment he is wishing he had not told me, and wondering if we are unsuited and if he should find some means of having our marriage contract revoked …

It was at that point in her meditation, that Catherine recognized the truth. She got up from her chair and, walking over to the window, looked across the terrace towards the walled and hidden rose-garden.

Why did I behave so childishly? she thought. Why did I react so foolishly to what he told me? There is only one answer. I am in love with him, deeply and irrevocably in love with him. I was consumed by jealousy when he told me of his lady-love and his bastard son, the more so when I realized that he had a genuine affection for the child.

And yet, in truth, is it not for those same attributes that caused me hurt and anger, that I love him? Do I love him less because of his honesty? Because he admits to an affection for his son?

In telling me the truth, he was demonstrating his love for me, his wish to ensure that no secret of his could mar our future happiness.

Oh, how deeply I regret my foolishness! I feel an urge to go to him now, to seek him out and tell him that nothing matters save our love for each other.

But nay, I must wait till the morrow. I shall contain my soul in patience till we meet in the rose-garden tomorrow afternoon. Then I shall admit my fault, and tell him without reservation of my love for him. Then all will be well, and life will be filled with joy and happiness and longing.

* * *

Catherine fell asleep almost as soon as her head touched the pillow that night. She awoke about four o'clock and lay warm and lethargic, gazing into the darkness.

It is curious, she thought, how everything has changed in the past two days. I seem to be seeing it all with different eyes. Lying here now, I think of the beauty of Kenninghall, instead of harking back to the homeliness of Sackville. I feel happy and safe – and loved in a way that I never did before.

I long for the day of my bridal, whereas before I viewed it with dread. I long to become truly my lord's bride and – though I would not so much as whisper the words aloud – the mother of his children.

Holy Mother be thanked, I am so happy and joyful now! Two days ago I would have dismissed such a possibility with scorn. I can scarcely wait till the morrow. I shall remain here in my chamber till the afternoon, trying to control my impatience, and then I shall go to meet my lord. At once I shall tell him of my love for him, and beg his forgiveness for yesterday's foolishness. Then, when I have assured him that all is well, perchance he will take me in his arms and kiss me …

She must have fallen asleep again at that point, for she remembered nothing more until she was awakened by the sound of one of the bed-curtains being drawn back.

"I'm sorry to disturb you at such an hour, my lady," Lucy was saying, "but His Lordship insists the matter is urgent, so I thought I'd better give you his message."

"Who says what is urgent?" asked Catherine drowsily, closing her eyes against the sudden brightness of hastily lit candles.

"Lord Thomas wishes to speak with you immediately, my lady. Alone, he says," Lucy added disapprovingly. "It seems he is shortly leaving Kenninghall and wishes to bid you farewell."

"Leaving Kenninghall?" asked Catherine, suddenly wide awake. "Now? What time is it?"

"Six o'clock, my lady."

"And my lord wishes to speak to me now?"

Lucy nodded. "And *alone*, my lady – I feel sure His Grace would not approve …"

But already Catherine was sitting up, and was plumping up the pillows and neatening the bedclothes.

"Pray fetch my negligée, Lucy, that I may be modestly attired to see my lord," she said firmly. "And then fetch my hair brush."

"Which negligée, my lady?" asked Lucy, still on a note of disapproval. "Your best one – the one trimmed with white fur?"

"Nay, the green silk."

"The green silk? But that is …"

"Unlucky," interposed Catherine impatiently. "Maybe it is, but I shall wear it just the same! Pray do not stand there gaping, Lucy. Please hurry."

A few minutes later, displaying an air of composure she was far from feeling, Catherine bade Lucy show her visitor in.

As Lord Thomas entered the chamber, Catherine noticed with a sinking heart that he was booted and spurred as if for a long journey. He was wearing thigh-length leather boots, a leather jerkin over his doublet, and a serviceable fur-lined cloak hung from his shoulders.

"I bid you a good morning, my lady," he said as, in response to Catherine's signal, Lucy reluctantly left the chamber, closing the door behind her. "I apologise for disturbing you at so early an hour. I considered leaving a letter for you, but could not bring myself to leave without seeing you to bid you farewell."

"But you said you would not be leaving for about a week, until after your sister's return, my lord." Catherine reminded him.

"Such was my intention – yesterday," he said. "At four o'clock this morning a messenger arrived from London. He had ridden all night to bring me my lord father's letter – a letter which has resulted in an immediate change of plan."

"Something is wrong, my lord?"

"Something is wrong," he said grimly. "Please God the matter is not too serious."

"Pray be seated, my lord," Catherine said, indicating a cushioned chair beside the bed, "and tell me what is amiss."

"It would seem that my sister's mischief-making was not confined to trying to cause a rift between you and me, my lady," he told her. "Her main purpose in going to London was to seek audience with His Majesty, her father-in-law, and, armed with information given her by Bess Holland, make damaging accusations against my father and brother."

"Mother of mercy!" exclaimed Catherine in horror. "Can this be true, my lord?"

"I fear there is little doubt of it," he told her.

"How did His Majesty receive the information?"

"It seems that he laughed her to scorn and dismissed her from his presence. But my father's enemies lost little time in turning my sister's rejected evidence to their advantage. Further evidence against my brother was supplied by those arch-fiends, Lord Hertford and his brother Sir Thomas Seymour. It was claimed that Henry had conceived a plan to murder certain members of the Privy Council prior to an attack on the monarchy itself."

"But surely, my lord, no one in their right mind would take such accusations seriously."

"So one might imagine," nodded Lord Thomas gravely. "Unfortunately His Majesty is a sick man, one who has aged beyond his fifty-six years, and he is plagued by anxiety over the succession. Prince Edward, his heir, is a sickly youth of sixteen summers. Doubtless His Majesty fears that, in the event of his own demise, my lord father, who – as well as being premier duke of England and leader of the Catholic faction – has a strong claim to the throne through his Plantagenet blood, will seize power. Lord Hertford and his brother are Prince Edward's uncles and could therefore be relied upon – so His Majesty reasons – to protect his interests."

"And would your lord father attempt to seize power?" asked Catherine watching his expression carefully.

"That I cannot say, my lady. My lord father is a law unto himself and keeps his own counsel," he admitted. "Only he – and Bess Holland perchance! – could answer that question. As to the Seymours, they are time-serving opportunists who protect only their own interests – Prince Edward would be no more than a puppet, alas, if they achieved power."

"Then your brother is in some danger following such allegations, my lord."

"He has been arrested on a charge of high treason," he told her quietly.

"Holy Mother!" exclaimed Catherine aghast. "Is it really so? Is the matter truly as serious as that?"

Lord Thomas nodded. "According to the information contained in my father's letter, my brother is in some danger – and he himself is under house arrest at the Howard mansion in Whitehall. His letter was conveyed to me in secret by a trusted manservant. My father asks me to go to London immediately and, since he will not be permitted to do so, give evidence in Henry's defence and act for him in all related matters."

"Could not you yourself be in danger also?" asked Catherine anxiously. "Especially if you speak in your brother's defence."

"Nay, sweeting." He smiled. "Have no fear – I shall come to no harm. I play no part in politics, as His Majesty is well aware. That fact will make me the better able to serve my family's interests at this time."

"What of Mary?" asked Catherine. "Where will she go? Surely, after what has transpired, she will not be returning to Kenninghall."

"The King has ordered that she and Bess Holland be placed under house arrest here at Kenninghall," explained Lord Thomas. "His Majesty is unconvinced of Mary's story, and is seeing to it that she and Bess Holland are kept under surveillance until it can be refuted or substantiated."

"Please God it will be the former," said Catherine fervently. "The charges against your brother must surely be false."

"The main charge – of plotting to overthrow the monarchy – is false: I would stake my life on that." Lord Thomas hesitated. "As to the charge of plotting to murder certain members of the Privy Council – namely Lord Hertford and his brother – I know not what to think, though I would admit it to none but you in whom I have complete trust."

"It is hard to believe that the Earl your brother would act so rashly, my lord."

"He hates Hertford and Tom Seymour – there can be no doubt of that. He sees them as low-born upstarts who, thanks to their sister's marriage to His Majesty, have used every means of influencing His Majesty against him. Since Hertford has recently replaced Henry as commander of the English forces in France, his hatred of Hertford has reached boiling point. Dearly as I love him, I cannot deny that Henry of Surrey is hot-headed to the point of rashness."

"What will be the outcome of it all, my lord?" Catherine's voice was troubled.

Lord Thomas shrugged. "Until I reach London and can judge for myself which way the wind blows, it is hard to say. At the worst, methinks Henry, and perhaps my lord father also, will be given a brief spell of imprisonment in the Tower – but for lesser charges than high treason."

"And what are those lesser charges, my lord?" asked Catherine curiously.

"Since his recent banishment to Mount Surrey, my brother has continued to act with his usual disregard for consequences. My lord father has more than once remonstrated with him about the matter – but to no avail."

"Of what do you speak, my lord?"

"My brother had alterations made to the quarterings in his escutcheon. In a new portrait of himself, his escutcheon is represented with the three silver labels from the Brotherton quarterings transferred to those of Edward the Confessor, thus implying that Henry of Surrey's maternal ancestors were directly descended from St. Edward and that he is therefore in the line of succession."

"And that is a serious offence, my lord?"

"In the present climate a dangerously serious offence. His Majesty could well see it as a deliberate provocation to himself, in that it suggests that the Howard family has a stronger claim to the throne than the Tudors."

"But is not that the case?" asked Catherine. "I once heard my lord father say as much."

"It is indeed the case – which makes Henry of Surrey's action dangerous to the point of foolhardiness! It appears that Henry's altered escutcheon has been the chief topic of conversation at Court for several weeks past. Till now, His Majesty has been ever indulgent of Henry's rash undertakings – he has fondly referred to his as 'the most foolish proud boy in England!' But this time, I fear, Henry has gone too far. He will be required to pay the penalty by imprisonment. My chief care in going to London will be to save my father from being blamed for Henry's misdeeds – I shall give evidence as to his disapproval and remonstrances over the altered escutcheon."

"Alas, my lord, I understand why you must go, but I shall miss you greatly!" sighed Catherine. "For the greater part of the time since my arrival here, we have been as strangers, and now, since we have discovered our regard for each other, we are to be parted. Alas for all those wasted days!"

He smiled suddenly. "Then I can take it that you were not too distressed by what I told you yesterday? That you do not see it as a hindrance to our future happiness?" he asked.

"Alas, my lord, I was very foolish yesterday. I realized it afterwards and was going to tell you so this afternoon. You were right to tell me, to make sure that no secret that might mar our happiness should lie between us. Last night I regretted my cool reception of your disclosure, and resolved to tell you so today. Now, alas, I regret it more than ever. Pray forgive me, my sweet lord."

"There is naught to forgive, beloved," he said tenderly. "You were hurt and shocked by my disclosure – I realized that. Now all is well. I shall leave here with a clear conscience, and with my heart full of gladness for the future."

"Oh, how I regret those wasted weeks!" sighed Catherine. "All the time you are away, I shall think of the words that are unsaid and the questions that are unanswered. I shall be tormented by anxiety for your safety, and by longing for your presence."

"God willing, we shall not be separated for long, beloved. Believe me, I shall be away no longer than it takes to achieve my purpose. I could be back here at Kenninghall in less than a fortnight."

"A fortnight! That sounds like a lifetime, my lord," pouted Catherine.

"It would then be a mere six weeks to our wedding day," he reminded her. "Think only of that and the time will soon pass."

"What if your return should be delayed? What if you are not back in time for our bridal?"

"Foolish one! Have no fear on that score. I shall be home long before then – think you I would delay making you mine, truly mine, for a single moment longer than I must?"

"Kiss me, my lord," Catherine said suddenly.

He seated himself on the bed and, taking one of her hands in his, bent forward and gently pressed his lips to the palm.

The kiss sent a ripple of pleasure coursing through her veins but, looking at him, she saw that his expression was sombre.

"There is something else I must say to you," he told her. "Mary will shortly be returning here under armed escort and both she and Bess Holland, as I explained, will be placed under house arrest. Kenninghall will not be a comfortable place to live in for a while, alas."

"I shall not mind – for myself," Catherine assured him. "I shall remain mostly in this chamber – though I might take a walk to the rose-garden, our own special place, now and then. You will be constantly in my thoughts, and I shall be wishing the time away till your return."

"You of course will not be affected by the presence of the guards. You are in no way involved in the present troubles – how could you be since you are still a Sackville, and your lord father, like myself, passes his time in rural pursuits rather than the intricacies of Court life?"

"What of Frances, my lord?" Catherine asked, suddenly.

"God forgive me, I was forgetting poor Frances – she will be distraught with anxiety when she learns what has befallen the Earl of Surrey. Methinks I should go to Mount Surrey, to keep her company and bid her take heart – indeed I shall ride over there this very morning."

"I absolutely forbid it," Lord Thomas said sternly. "There are complications enough at the present time."

"But you yourself said I was in no way involved, my lord."

"That is so," he nodded. "All the same, my lady, I insist that you remain here unless I direct otherwise. You are not involved, as I said – but should you go to Mount Surrey now, such a visit could well be misinterpreted."

"But, my lord, I am very fond of Frances – is it not natural that I should wish to see her now? Surely no ill could come of such a visit. She is six months with child and must be greatly in need of consolation."

"I had hoped to spare you such news, but you leave me no choice, my lady: Frances and her children are already under house arrest."

"Sweet Jesus have pity!" exclaimed Catherine fervently. "But what has Frances done, my lord? She has surely not been involved in your brother's intrigues!"

"Frances is my brother's wife. Since he is charged with the most serious crime of all, high treason, she too must remain under surveillance." Lord Thomas hesitated as if loth to express himself further. "Should things go badly with my brother, as God forbid, Frances will seek the protection of her father, the Earl of Oxford."

"You said just now that I must remain here – unless you direct otherwise. What meant you, my lord?"

"I meant nothing in particular." He spoke lightly, but Catherine noticed that he avoided meeting her gaze. "It was but a generalisation. Should my absence be prolonged, as is highly unlikely, or should I deem it wise to separate you from the combined influence of my sister and Bess Holland, I would contact your lord father."

"To what purpose, my lord?"

"I should ask him to make arrangements to take you back to Sackville Hall until the commotion is past."

"Then you suspect that you yourself may be in danger," Catherine said fearfully.

"I am a Howard and, as such, I shall remain loyal and true

to my family, come what may. But as I told you, my lady, I am in no way involved in the political intrigues of my father and brother. Should I make such a request to your father, it would be solely out of a natural concern for the maiden I love more than life itself."

"Whatever the outcome of your visit to London, I would rather wait for you here, my lord," Catherine told him.

Is that the truth? she thought in surprise. Three days ago I would have danced for joy at the possibility of returning to Sackville. Now, at the mere thought of leaving Kenninghall, my eyes mist with tears and I am overwhelmed by sadness. In truth, it is not the thought of leaving Kenninghall that is so distressing, but the implications – the realization that my lord himself could be in some danger.

"It makes little difference whether you wait for me here or at Sackville, my lady," Lord Thomas was saying. "Once the matter has been satisfactorily resolved, I shall come to you immediately wherever you are. My duty and loyalty are to my family, but my love and devotion are all for you."

"Must you go so soon, my lord? 'Tis not yet daylight ..."

"Fifteen minutes from now my men-at-arms will be mounting up ready for departure," he interposed. "I myself am ready for the journey but, since there will be no other Howard here at Kenninghall once I have departed, there are matters to be attended to first."

"Matters such as Bess Holland, my lord?" she asked. "She knows not of your departure?"

"Nay, I gave orders that she was not to be informed. I shall have to choose my words carefully in speaking to her, for it is imperative that she knows as little as possible of the reason for my sudden departure. It would be preferable for her to remain ignorant of the outcome of her treachery until Mary's return!"

"Be assured, my lord, that she will learn nothing from me," Catherine told him.

"I know that, beloved."

"Pray kiss me, my lord." Catherine held out her arms to him. "On my lips this time."

He leaned forward and kissed her tenderly, and then

handed her a small silk-wrapped package he had been holding.

"A parting gift for my lady Greensleeves," he said.

Smiling excitedly, Catherine untied the ribbon and carefully unwrapped the package.

"Oh, 'tis beautiful, my lord," she said, gazing down at the gold pendant set with diamonds and emeralds that sparkled in the flickering candlelight. "So very beautiful – how good you are to me, my lord!"

"I had it wrought specially for you," he told her. "The goldsmith finished it only yesterday – in the nick of time, as it were! Green is your colour, my lady – that is why I chose emeralds. You were wearing a green gown on that first day I saw you, and this morning you are again attired in a green that matches your eyes."

"My lord, is it true that some in these parts consider it unlucky for a maiden to wear green?" asked Catherine. "Lucy tells me it is so, and that only a married lady may wear green in safety!"

"I have heard the superstition," smiled Lord Thomas. "But I pay no heed to such things."

"My lord, I know I am not suitably attired for such splendour," Catherine said, placing the fine gold chain that held the pendant, around her neck, "but I cannot wait to see how it looks. Pray fasten the clasp for me."

He bent forward and fastened the clasp and sat back to survey the result.

"The goldsmith is a true craftsman," he said, "and your beauty, my lady, serves to enhance his handiwork."

For one long moment they gazed at each other in silence, a moment when each could only guess what was in the other's mind.

Suddenly, Catherine reached out long slender arms and clasped them around his neck.

"Kiss me again, my lord," she said tremulously. "I love you with all my heart, and know not how I shall endure the next two weeks without you."

He kissed her passionately on the lips, and she drew him fiercely towards her.

"Hold me close, my lord, and kiss me again and again," she murmured.

He drew back and gazed down at her, his dark eyes inscrutable and strangely exciting.

"You tempt me almost beyond endurance," he said, his voice vibrant with emotion. "To hold you and kiss you as you wish – as we both wish – with our hearts beating as one and heavy with the sorrow of our parting, would be too much. Methinks kissing alone would not suffice either of us."

"My lord, I care not …"

"Greatly as you tempt me, beloved, I will not take you till you are rightfully mine," he interposed. "Eight weeks from now, you will come to me as a virgin bride."

"You are right, my lord," she murmured, her eyes brimming with tears. "Of course you are right. Pray forgive my forwardness – it was prompted solely by my love for you."

"I know that," he said gently. "Believe me, sweeting, I know how you feel. But I shall wait for you with single-mindedness and longing."

"Then this is farewell, my lord," she said, trying unsuccessfully to keep the tremor from her voice.

He kissed her lightly on the lips.

"It is indeed," he said softly, placing a hand on one of her breasts – a gentle caress that set her body aflame with a desire she was unable fully to comprehend. "I shall think of you night and day."

"And I of you, my sweet lord," she whispered. "May Our Lady have you always in her blessed protection."

"Farewell, beloved," he said, getting resolutely to his feet, and fastening the jewelled clasp of his cloak as he moved towards the door.

His booted footsteps echoed back from the walls of the passageway outside, and Catherine listened until the sounds had receded into silence.

For a long time after he had gone, Catherine lay still and silent in her bed. Dry-eyed now, she nevertheless knew a disturbing sense of foreboding.

My lord was more concerned than he wished me to know,

she thought. He was concerned for his father and brother –
that is understandable. But he was concerned also for me.
Was he trying to keep the true gravity of the situation from
me, by making light of his own endeavour in giving evidence in
favour of his kinsmen? In seeking to help them, is not he
placing himself at risk?

I sensed an uneasiness in my lord when I asked him of the
superstition about a maiden wearing the colour green. He
spoke lightly and smiled when I asked him of it, and yet still I
sensed his disquiet. Perchance it was tactless of me to ask him
of it at such a time – and when he had given me so beautiful a
gift.

Her fingers fastened on the pendant which still lay on her
white throat, and she felt the cold hardness of the jewels. 'Tis
strange how easily I recall the verse Lucy told me! she
thought.

She murmured the words aloud:

"Wear a green kirtle before you be wed
And you'll have no husband to warm your bed
So put on your blue, your russet, or red,
Or still be a maid on the day you're dead."

Why, oh why, must I dwell on that now? she thought. All
these weeks I have scarcely given it a thought and now I am
suddenly reminded of it.

Is it in truth unlucky for a maiden to wear green? Is my
lord's gift, given to me at our farewell and reminding me of the
superstition, an ill-omen? I must try not to think thus. I am
affected by the unexpectedness of my lord's departure, by the
knowledge that he has departed on a mission that could be
fraught with danger to himself.

Will I ever see him again? she asked herself in sudden
anguish. Was this a final farewell? I can hear the horses
stamping their feet down below in the courtyard. I hear the
clinking of harness and the shouts of the men-at-arms as they
mount up ready for departure, and now comes the command
to move off ...

Every passing moment is taking my lord further away from me. Quietly and resolutely, he is moving towards intrigues and perils I could not begin to imagine.

I could be back here at Kenninghall in less than a fortnight: those were my lord's words. He could be back, but *will* he be back by then?

Why do I have this terrifying sense of foreboding? 'Tis as if, at my lord's departure, the light has gone from Kenninghall, leaving me in permanent darkness.

This great house is staffed by upwards of two hundred servants and yet, without its masters, it is naught but an empty shell. With my lord's departure, the last of the Howards has gone – and it seems to me that the heart of Kenninghall has gone with him.

Fourteen

Mary, Duchess of Richmond, arrived back at Kenninghall with her entourage two weeks after Lord Thomas's departure.

Catherine had heard nothing of Lord Thomas in the meantime and, on being informed by Lucy of Mary's arrival, wondered if Mary could give her news of him. But aware as she was of Mary's disloyalty to her family and her propensity for mischief-making, she quelled the urge to go to her apartment and ask her for information about her younger brother.

Guards had been posted at all the outside doors, both to prevent Mary and Bess Holland from leaving Kenninghall and to interrogate any unknown arrivals, but everyone was free to move at will within the confines of the house.

If Mary wishes to speak to me, thought Catherine, there is nothing to prevent her doing so, though Lucy tells me she went straight to her apartment on her arrival and has remained there ever since, refusing to see anyone but her personal maid.

"Her maid, Bessie, says Her Ladyship's being more difficult than usual," Lucy had said, "and that's saying something! One moment she's in one of her tantrums, and the next she's lying on her bed weeping! I'd not be in poor Bessie's shoes, my lady!"

"I expect Lady Mary is still feeling the effects of the journey," said Catherine. "It teemed with rain for the whole two days, I understand."

"I said as much to Bessie, my lady, but she shook her head," Lucy told her. " 'Nay,' she said, 'Her Ladyship's been up to something, that's certain. She rants and raves about the

King – it seems he sent her away with a flea in her ear!' ''

* * *

It was not until the following afternoon that Mary went to Catherine's chamber.

Catherine greeted her amicably enough, having resolved to say nothing of what Lord Thomas had told her unless Mary herself made reference to it. But, anxious for news of the man she loved, she found it no easy matter to maintain her resolve.

"So you are still here, Catherine," Mary said lightly, as she entered the chamber. "By the Mass! In your place, I should have turned and fled back to Dorset and sanity long since!"

"You look well, Mary," Catherine said in surprise, ignoring the taunt. "You look no different from when you went away."

"You say the oddest things, Catherine!" Mary's voice was mocking. "Did you imagine I would have changed in a few weeks? Did you expect me to have become an old hag overnight?"

What did I expect? Catherine thought to herself. Did I imagine her treachery would show? In spite of what Lucy told me, she looks untroubled. Does not she suffer guilt at what she has done? Had I acted in such a way, I feel sure that guilt would be written all over me! Indeed I believe I could not live with the shame if I had played traitor to my family and placed their lives in jeopardy.

"I was referring to your journey," she managed to say coolly. "Despite the long, wearisome journey from London, you look fresh as a daisy."

"I long since slept away the tiredness of the journey," Mary told her. "What else is there to do but sleep in this great mausoleum?"

"Mausoleum? A mausoleum is a tomb – what makes you refer to Kenninghall thus?"

"It may not be a tomb – yet!" said Mary pointedly. "But a prison it most certainly is! Have not you heard the news?"

"What news?" asked Catherine, trying to hide her sudden interest.

"Poor Lady Mary has been placed under house arrest – by His Majesty's command. What do you think of that, little Catherine? Can you credit it? – the old lecher has had his daughter-in-law confined to barracks! I know 'tis a mere formality and that I shall only remain thus whilst enquiries are being made as to the extent of my kinsmen's treasonable conduct – but it is vexing!"

"I know not what you mean, my lady," said Catherine. "To which of your kinsmen were you referring?"

"My father and my brother Henry – who else?" demanded Mary. "Or were you wondering if dear Tom was in league with them?"

"I know nothing of politics and suchlike," said Catherine, with a nonchalance she was far from feeling. "And of course I know you do not mean me to take such words seriously. Mistress Holland also is under house arrest, I understand."

"Bess? Did she tell you that?" Mary asked, suspiciously.

"Nay, she has made no mention of it. But 'tis common knowledge here at Kenninghall, is it not? Mistress Holland comes here each morning, as always, to enquire as to my welfare and requirements, but she stays for only a few minutes."

"There is an edge to your voice when you speak of her," Mary said thoughtfully. "Do not you approve of her?"

"It is not for me to approve or disapprove," Catherine said evasively. "She seems to be an excellent housekeeper."

"I really must have a talk with Bess. I thought it unwise, in the circumstances, for us to be seen together immediately after my return, but she must be dying for news." Mary looked tauntingly at Catherine. "And what of you, Catherine? Are not you dying for news?"

"For news?" asked Catherine blankly.

"Are not you beside yourself with curiosity as to what has befallen my father and brothers?" persisted Mary. "How strange that you have not asked!"

"Have you knowledge then of their present situation? I naturally assumed that you were still at Richmond at the time of the Earl of Surrey's arrest in London, and it would have been tactless to speak of it till you yourself did so."

"Dear Catherine!" mocked Mary. "Always so tactful and innocent, are you not?"

"Then you have news of the Duke and the Earl?"

"Henry is to be sent for trial on a charge of high treason," Mary told her. "And my father is at present held prisoner in the Tower while fresh evidence is being brought to light."

"And what of Lord Thomas?" Catherine spoke with a lightness that belied her anxiety.

"Tom?" Mary smiled tantalisingly. "I wondered how long it would take you to ask about him! You see, Catherine, you were wrong in thinking I remained at Richmond throughout my absence. For the past two weeks, I have been under house arrest at the Howard mansion in Whitehall – in returning to Kenninghall, I merely exchanged one prison for another."

"And what has this to do with my lord Thomas?" asked Catherine carelessly.

"It was there, at the house in Whitehall, that I saw Tom," explained Mary. "Like a dutiful son, he had journeyed all the way from Norfolk to see what he could do to help his poor, misunderstood old father!"

"*And* his poor, misunderstood elder brother," put in Catherine. "Let us not forget him."

"Him too," nodded Mary. "Methinks you are already acquainted with the situation. Dear me! I shall have to watch my step!"

"You were about to tell me of my lord Thomas." Catherine reminded her.

"So I was! Well, you see, Catherine, dear Thomas is not at all pleased with his little sister. He spoke to me no more than was absolutely necessary during the time we were living under the same roof at Whitehall – and when he did bring himself to speak to me, there was a coldness in his eyes and a hardness in his voice that quite gave me the shivers!"

"Doubtless he had his reasons."

"Doubtless," agreed Mary. "All the same, Catherine, you'd best give thought to the matter. Your betrothed could well be a cold bridegroom – never say I didn't warn you! Come to think of it – and judging by the way you are looking at me at this moment – you could be well suited!''

"What did my lord Thomas say when he did speak to you?" enquired Catherine, ignoring the gibes with some difficulty.

"He told me that father and Henry were in grave peril – from the way he spoke, one might have imagined he was blaming me for their misfortune." Mary sighed ostentatiously. "Heigh-ho! One cannot be everybody's favourite!"

"And that was all he said?"

"All? Had you been there and heard what he said and how he said it, you would realize it was more than enough," Mary told her. "Oh, he mentioned you, of course."

"Indeed?"

"He told me that, during my absence, you and he had formed 'a close attachment,' as he put it," Mary laughed in reminiscence. " 'I trust not *too* close an attachment, brother!' I said. With that, he gave me such a look that I still cannot decide if it was prompted by guilt or frustration."

"Or anger?" suggested Catherine.

"Anger?" Mary considered the question. "That could be it – but what could you possibly have done to anger him, Catherine?"

"He said nothing else?" Catherine managed to ask. "He gave you no message for me?"

"Nay, he gave me no message. Do you know, Catherine, I almost had the impression that dear Thomas would not entirely trust me to convey a message? Would you believe that? What is the world coming to, when a brother does not trust his own sister?"

"What indeed!" said Catherine whole-heartedly.

"He even went so far as to give me a warning," complained Mary.

"A warning?"

"He warned me about you."

"About me? Why should he warn you against me?" demanded Catherine. "I suppose this is another sample of your mischief-making."

"Alas, Catherine, how could you speak thus!" said Mary

reproachfully. "Are we not friends, you and I? You really must listen more attentively – I said that Tom warned me about you, not against you."

"Pray tell me what he said, my lady."

"He said that if I should do anything whatsoever to cause you harm, he would throttle me with his own hands." Mary's expression was one of wide-eyed innocence. "Now I ask you, Catherine dear, is that a nice way for a brother to talk to his sister? Would your brother speak so to you?"

"My brother would never have cause to speak to me thus," Catherine said pointedly.

"And you think that Tom has?"

"I did not say that," Catherine said quietly. "Only you can answer that question."

But Mary's question, it seemed, had been rhetorical, for she gave no heed to Catherine's reply. Occupied with her own thoughts, her carefree manner had undergone a change.

She looked suddenly fearful, as if the light-heartedness had been only a pose.

Perchance her conscience troubles her more than she will admit – even to herself! thought Catherine. She looks curiously vulnerable, as if her brother's words touched some chord in her memory that awakened guilt.

" 'I will throttle you with my own hands.' Those were my brother's very words." Mary's face was pale and tense. "And do you know, Catherine, I would swear he meant what he said."

"I feel sure you are taking his words too seriously," Catherine told her. " 'Tis true that, during your absence, Lord Thomas and I discovered our mutual regard. Believe me, Mary, I love him dearly and long for his return. He doubtless realized I would be concerned by his continuing absence – and feared that on your return you would try to cause a rift between us."

"As if I would do such a thing!" Mary said, indignantly.

"There was the little matter of your lovelorn brother and the squire's daughter – remember? There was also the matter of my tragic parting from another squire's son – you remember that also, do you not?"

"So you found out!" chuckled Mary. "Really, Catherine, you are a goose – you were quite taken in by my little tale, were you not?"

"That then probably explains your brother's concern," said Catherine.

Mary looked at her for a few moments, and Catherine saw that again her expression had changed. Her smile had vanished, and her face was melancholy and brooding.

"You are wrong, Catherine," she said slowly. "Though I like it not, I am a Howard – it takes a Howard to understand a Howard at times. Thomas keeps his feelings well hidden, but he would fight to the death for his rights and principles – and for the maiden he loves!"

"I have never heard you speak like this before," Catherine said in surprise. "Perchance you over-reacted to what your brother said – it was surely not meant to be taken literally."

"Oh, but it was, Catherine," insisted Mary. "Indeed it was. I confess I was surprised – even shocked – by the strength of his feelings. Can this be Tom, my reserved, even-tempered brother? I asked myself, I realized then that I had never truly known him – it was as if he were a stranger."

"No doubt he was distressed by the news of his father and brother, and spoke hastily," Catherine said reassuringly.

"Nay, Catherine, he meant what he said all right," insisted Mary, and Catherine was surprised to see tears in her eyes. "Thomas, I have discovered, is a man of passion. He loves with passion, and hates with equal passion. He loves you and he hates me. He is a man of fire and ice. Why did I never see him so before?"

Fifteen

Catherine received an unexpected caller on the morning that followed Mary's return.

"You have a visitor, my lady," Lucy told her.

"I assume you are referring to Lady Mary," Catherine said, aware of conflicting reactions to the information. "Show her in, Lucy."

"Nay, 'tis not Lady Mary. This visitor is not of the household – she's not even of the nobility." There was no mistaking Lucy's disapproval. "Her husband farms land about two miles from here."

"Then what can she want with me? I expect it is Mistress Holland she wishes to see – I expect she has dairy produce to sell."

"She insists it's you she wants to see, my lady. She's harmless enough, poor soul, or the guards wouldn't have let her past the door."

"Poor soul, you say?"

"She's near her time with child, my lady," explained Lucy. "That brute of a husband of hers gets her in the family way each year as regular as clockwork."

"You know her, of course," said Catherine, recalling that Lucy had lived all her life in the nearby village and knew the inhabitants for several miles around.

"Her name's Drusilla Benson, my lady," Lucy told her with notable reluctance. "Perchance you've heard of her."

"Why should I have heard of her?" asked Catherine curiously. "Until a few weeks ago, I had lived always in Dorset."

"All the same, my lady ..." Lucy's sentence tailed off significantly.

"Are you trying to tell me something, Lucy? Is Drusilla Benson a woman of low repute or something?"

"I'd not say that, my lady, though she was once the subject of a village scandal." Lucy's tone was uncustomarily evasive. "Before she married Jake Benson, she lived at *The White Lion* in Norwich – she's the daughter of Daniel Gurney, the innkeeper."

"*The White Lion?*" asked Catherine thoughtfully.

"Dan Gurney had three daughters and, one way and another, they all earned themselves a bit of a reputation," explained Lucy. "They were all pretty, but Drusilla was the prettiest and the youngest – she was the prettiest maiden in these parts and was chosen to be May Queen."

"That must surely have been before your time, Lucy," said Catherine, recalling Lord Thomas telling her that his bastard was the grandson of the innkeeper at Norwich.

"A bit before," admitted Lucy. "The scandal started about eight years ago."

"Well, now I know who Drusilla Benson is, the next step is to find out why she wishes to see me," said Catherine. "So pray show her in."

"And the boy, my lady?"

"The boy?"

"She's brought one of her children with her."

"Then show them both in," said Catherine on a note of exasperation.

In truth she was curious to know what Drusilla Benson, a farmer's wife, could want with her. Why is Lucy acting so strangely? she thought to herself as the girl left the chamber. Could it be that Drusilla Benson is the daughter who – who ... The subject of a village scandal, Lucy said. Is it possible that she is ...? Nay, I am thinking foolishly. What could a person like that want with me?

The woman who entered the chamber looked ordinary enough. Can this be she of whom Lucy was speaking? Catherine thought to herself. Is it possible that she was the village beauty a mere eight years ago? Nay, this woman is nearing forty, it is clear. Her blue eyes look tired and faded and there is a strand or two of silver in her hair. Still, no woman looks her best when she is near her time and she is plainly that. Apart from her belly though, she looks thin and frail as if the child she is carrying has drained her strength.

The newcomer curtsied awkwardly, and thankfully accepted Catherine's offer of a chair.

"You are Mistress Benson, I understand," Catherine said then. "My maid tells me you brought your son with you – do not you wish to bring him in here?"

"'Tis best he waits outside in the passageway, my lady, if you please," Mistress Benson said nervously. "I'd rather speak what's in my mind to you alone."

"Tell me what I can do for you, Mistress Benson," Catherine said graciously. "But first I will ring for some refreshment."

"After, my lady, if you please. Let me tell you what's in my mind before my courage fails me."

"Pray continue," smiled Catherine encouragingly. "But please take your time, since there is no necessity for haste."

"Forgive me, my lady, but there is need for haste. You see, it took James and me three quarters of an hour to get here, me being in the family way, and I've left my other children at home."

"They are surely not on their own," said Catherine anxiously.

"The cowman will keep an eye on them for me and see they don't come to harm, but I must be back home before my husband returns for his dinner."

"You mean you walked all that way in your condition – Lucy tells me you live two miles away."

Mistress Benson nodded. "I'm used enough to walking, my lady. But my legs are a bit swelled up at the moment – with the babby I suppose – and that makes me walk a bit slow."

"Then I shall ring for some hot milk and cakes, and you can sit quietly and tell me what I can do for you," said Catherine, ringing the bell for a servant. "Afterwards I will have one of the grooms drive you home in the pony cart."

"Nay, my lady, that would never do. Whether you answer yea or nay to what I'm about to ask of you, still it would never do. Folk gossip in these parts – they don't forget easily, nor do they let others forget neither. If Drusilla Benson was to be seen being driven home by one of the Kenninghall servants, 'twould be all over the village by nightfall."

"What if it were?" smiled Catherine. "Surely no one would begrudge your being driven home – in the circumstances!"

"My husband is a jealous man, my lady," sighed Mistress Benson. "If he discovered I'd been here today, he'd put two and two together and make a dozen – and then he'd give me such a trouncing I'd fear for the babby."

"You mean he would beat you?" Catherine asked, incredulously.

"He'd beat me all right, my lady – there's no doubt of that."

"Surely not – no man in his senses would beat a woman with child!"

"With respect, my lady, you're young and you've a lot to learn about men and life I daresay."

"By criminy! It scarcely seems possible," declared Catherine. "Farmer Benson must be something of a brute. When do you expect your child?"

"Two weeks from now, my lady, and glad I'll be – given me a lot of trouble this one has."

"I expect it goes hard with you having a child at your age – and you already have six others, Lucy tells me," Catherine said sympathetically. "Kindly let me know when the child is born, Mistress Benson – I should like to visit you if I may and bring a gift for the baby."

Mistress Benson shook her head. "That isn't possible, my lady, though I thank you kindly for the thought. When I've told you what brings me here, you'll see why it isn't possible. But tell me first: you spoke just then of my age – how old do you think I am?"

Catherine hesitated. "Thirty-four – thirty-five at the outside," she said tactfully.

"The years have certainly taken their toll," Mistress

Benson said sadly. "Funny, but I haven't taken a really good look at myself for years – always been too busy I suppose! You see, my lady, I had James, my eldest, he who waits outside, seven years ago when I was sixteen."

"Then you are only twenty-three," said Catherine, unable to hide her astonishment. "But ... Pray forgive me, Mistress Benson, I ..."

"There is no need to apologise, my lady," interposed Mistress Benson with a rueful smile. "I know I look older. Life isn't always kind to us women."

"You are naturally weary from carrying the child and from your walk here today. Once you have had the baby, you will soon regain your youth and beauty."

"Beauty?"

"Lucy told me you were renowned as the village beauty."

"I was May Queen one year – that was when I was fifteen, the year before James was born."

A servant came in at that moment and Catherine waited while her visitor was served with refreshments.

"James is your eldest, Mistress Benson?" she asked then.

"He's my eldest, though not my husband's eldest," Mistress Benson explained. "James was not sired by my husband, you see. The boy is a bastard."

For a few moments there was silence in the chamber as Mistress Benson met Catherine's gaze and held it, telling Catherine without words all she needed to know.

"I see," Catherine said in a small voice.

"My lady, I know I've no right to ask your help, but I've come here today because I know not what else to do. The midwife has told me, and I believe she's right, that I'll not survive the birth of this child. Should I die, my husband in his grief would see James as the cause of his misfortunes and James would not long survive me."

"Let us speak plainly, Mistress Benson," Catherine said quietly. "I believe that James's father is a gentleman well known to me. Is it not so?"

Mistress Benson nodded. "He's the bastard of your betrothed, my lady. I know this must be a shock to you, but then all noblemen have their bastards and His Lordship is no exception."

"My lord told me of his bastard," said Catherine. "So let us keep to the practicalities. What makes you think I will help you?"

"You are a good woman, my lady, and will do what is right," was the simple answer.

"How do you know that?"

"I didn't know it before I came here today, my lady. Now I am certain of it. You will do what you can for my son."

"I understood from my lord that he and his father, the Duke of Norfolk, had made a generous settlement for James with your father."

"That is so, my lady," nodded Mistress Benson. "His Lordship made a generous settlement to my father – a sum large enough to exceed his expectations. He pays a further sum annually for the boy's upkeep."

"Then I fail to understand why you are here, Mistress Benson."

"After James was born, father married me off to Jake Benson – he himself had married again and didn't want me and James cluttering up the place, as he said," explained Mistress Benson. "He paid my husband part of the settlement as my dowry."

"I still do not see why …"

"How could you, my lady?" interposed Mistress Benson. "Doubtless you have been sheltered from the rogues and scoundrels of this world, the sort who use and abuse a helpless woman and an innocent child."

"You refer to Viscount Bindon?" asked Catherine white-faced.

Mistress Benson shook her head. "Nay, my lady. His Lordship is a gallant and honourable gentleman, one who pays his debts with generosity and kindness. I was referring, alas, to my own father and husband."

"Why so?"

"My husband is a jealous man – oh, he's fond of me in his own way, though many would find that hard to believe if they saw my bruised body at times," said Mistress Benson bitterly. "I fear he will vent his jealousy on James if I should die in childbed. With this in mind, I went yesterday to beg my father to promise that, if aught happens to me, he will take James under his protection. He refused. I reminded him of his settlement with the Duke and His Lordship, and of the money he is paid annually for James's upkeep, of which he pays my husband only a portion."

"What did he say to that?"

"He laughed at me. I long ago learned that it is when my father laughs that he is most dangerous. 'What settlement?' he asked. 'What upkeep? I've seen naught of any settlement. You got yourself in spawn, lass, and I found you a husband – paid him well too – to give you and the boy a home. That was the end of the matter as far as I was concerned.' 'And what will you say to His Lordship if harm befalls James and me?' I asked. 'What will you tell the Duke if he enquires about his grandson?'"

"How did he answer you?" asked Catherine.

"He laughed again," Mistress Benson told her. " 'Neither the Duke nor his sons are in a position to ask questions at the present time and, if you want my opinion, the Duke's days are numbered,' he said. 'If he and that rakehell son of his, young Surrey, escape from their present situation with their lives, 'twill be a miracle.'"

"Did not you remind him that His Lordship is James's father and that he himself is not in danger?" enquired Catherine.

"I did, my lady, but still the old devil laughed. 'The Duke's been accused of treason and if he's beheaded, as folks in these parts believe he will be, all his possessions will be forfeited to the Crown,' he said. 'If that happens, do you think his younger son will have nothing better to do than wander all over the countryside checking up on his bastards? Nay, daughter, he'll be too busy trying to keep himself from a debtors' prison, believe me.'"

"A debtors' prison," repeated Catherine faintly, this aspect of the situation not having occurred to her. "It will not come to that – it cannot come to that!"

Mistress Benson watched her shrewdly. "Then you will help me, my lady? For His Lordship's sake?"

"Why do you say that?"

Mistress Benson ignored the question. "My James is a good lad, an honest, affectionate lad. I beg you to take him into your care till His Lordship returns and can decide what is best for him," she said.

"I will consider the matter of course, but ..."

"I'm asking to take him now, my lady," interposed Mistress Benson.

"Now?" asked Catherine in surprise.

"Today. I'm asking to leave him here with you – for his safety and protection. Should I die, he would not long survive me – you can be sure of that, my lady."

"But there are no children here at Kenninghall at present – questions would be asked – it scarcely seems fitting for my lord's bastard to ..." Catherine was speaking her thoughts aloud. "What would His Lordship say if he returned to find your son here with me, Mistress Benson?"

"When he learned what had befallen in his absence, he would bless you for your charity, my lady," Mistress Benson told her tearfully. "As I do."

"I don't know what to say. You see, Mistress Benson, I have no experience of such matters. Perchance I should consult my lord's sister, the Duchess of Richmond."

"Pray don't do that, my lady," Mistress Benson said anxiously. "She doesn't know about James. His Lordship never told her he had a bastard – he told me that he and his father preferred to keep the knowledge from her."

Realizing that he would indeed have wished to keep the matter secret from his mischief-making sister, Catherine nodded.

"You are right," she said. "Had the Duchess known of James's existence, she would have told me of it by now."

"Perchance you doubt my story. Perchance you doubt that James is truly His Lordship's bastard ..."

"Nay, I no more doubt that than does His Lordship," interposed Catherine.

"Then you wonder if James is truly in danger?"

Catherine ignored the question. "I would like to see him,"

she said quietly.

"I will summon him, my lady," Mistress Benson got laboriously to her feet. "He is waiting at the end of the passageway."

As she left the chamber, Catherine was a prey to misgiving. Her curiosity to see the child of the man she loved, fought for predominance with her resentment of him. James, a bastard, was her lord's firstborn – the son she would have hoped to give him.

Her first sight of James as he followed his mother through the doorway satisfied her curiosity and, inexplicably, overcame her resentment.

She stared in astonishment. There could be no possible doubt of his paternity. My lord must have looked just like that at his son's age, she thought to herself.

"So you are James," she said with a smile, recollecting herself with an effort. "Your mother has been telling me of you."

The boy caught his mother's eye and bowed awkwardly, but made no reply. He gazed at Catherine with large brown eyes that reminded her forcibly of his father.

"Like His Lordship, isn't he, my lady?" Mistress Benson's voice clearly expressed her pride in her son. "Got the makings of a nobleman, hasn't he? My husband sees it too, alas, and complains that James gives himself airs."

"How would you like to stay here at Kenninghall for a few weeks, James?" asked Catherine in sudden decision.

"Stay here?" asked the boy in astonishment. "Stay here and run errands for you, you mean? I'd like that – if mama can spare me for a while. I'm good at collecting firewood."

"Of course I can spare you, James," Mistress Benson assured him cheerfully. "It would be one less mouth to feed and would give me a bit of peace at home till the baby's born – you and your stepfather are scarcely the best of friends!"

"Then that is settled," said Catherine.

"When can I come?" asked the boy.

"Now, if your mother agrees," Catherine told him, giving no hint of her conversation with Mistress Benson. "But you would not be here to run errands – I understand we have enough firewood for the time being. You would be treated like one of the family – it would be a sort of holiday for you."

"One of the family? But why …?" James was plainly puzzled. "But what of you, mama? How would you manage without me to help you look after the others, and fetch firewood and things? And – and …"

"And what, my son?"

"How would you manage to walk all the way home without me to look after you?" he asked anxiously.

There were tears in Mistress Benson's eyes, Catherine noticed. "Bless you, child! 'Tisn't right you should concern yourself about such things at your age! I'll manage well enough. I'll miss you of course, but I'll be happy knowing you're here and away from your stepfather's heavy hand."

"How long can I stay here?" James asked Catherine.

"Until His Lordship …" Catherine started to reply but Mistress Benson forestalled her.

"Until the baby's born, James," she told him. "I'll send word to you then and, as soon as Her Ladyship wishes it, you can return home. Meanwhile you must obey Her Ladyship in all things, just as you would obey me. Do you understand?"

"Yes, mama," nodded the boy soberly. "But I'll miss you. I've never been away from home before."

"Then it's about time you were," his mother said practically. "You're a very lucky boy to have such an opportunity!"

"Do you know, James, until a few weeks ago I had never been away from my home in Dorset," Catherine told him. "So I know what it is like to miss one's home – you and I will be able to cheer each other up when we feel homesick!"

Mistress Benson turned to Catherine. "If it's all right with you, my lady, I'll be on my way now. I'm feeling rested and that hot milk went down a treat!"

"Can I persuade you to change your mind about being driven home in the pony cart?" asked Catherine. "You would reach home quickly and with no effort at all."

"I'll be all right, my lady, really I will – though I thank you kindly for the offer. Knowing James is safe here with you will take a weight off my mind anyway. I can't tell you how grateful I am."

"He is a son to be proud of, Mistress Benson," Catherine told her, as she rang for a servant to show her visitor out.

"You love him, don't you?" said Mistress Benson, as if stating a fact.

"James, you mean? I ..."

"I was meaning His Lordship. I could see it in your expression when you spoke of him. Bless you both, my lady, you and His Lordship. I wish you every happiness."

"You do not blame him?"

"What is there to blame him for?" shrugged Mistress Benson. "He gave me my beloved son and he accepted responsibility for him with great willingness."

"You never harboured thoughts of marriage?"

"With him?" Mistress Benson smiled and shook her head. "Nay, my lady. He and I are from different worlds – I always recognized that. I'd be lost in a great house like this. I'd not know what to say or who to say it to. Nay, the past is no more than a dream now, a wonderful dream."

"You did love him though?" asked Catherine. "Forgive me, Mistress Benson, but it seems important that I know."

Mistress Benson hesitated. "I can't answer that question, my lady, in the way that you mean it. It seems to me there are different ways of loving, but in the long run most of us are happiest among our own kind. That's why James will never truly fit in at the farm. His stepfather knows that, though he couldn't put it into words. James is not our kind – I realize that, love him as I do. He's his father's kind."

"He is certainly that in appearance," smiled Catherine. "Have no fear, Mistress Benson. I shall take good care of him, whatever the future holds."

"I know you will. You're a good lass – er – my lady, and you've set my mind at ease. When His Lordship returns, then it'll be up to him to decide about the future." Mistress Benson turned to James who, not understanding the conversation, had been surveying the sumptuously furnished chamber with interest. "Farewell, my son. Do as Her Ladyship tells you and you'll come to no harm."

"I will, mama, but ..." James hesitated as if, after all, he would have preferred to go home. "But you'll let me know as soon as the baby's been born, won't you?"

"You'll hear soon enough," said his mother with a cheerfulness she was far from feeling. She hugged him to her and then moved determinedly towards the door and the waiting servant. "Go with God, my son – always."

"That's what His Lordship ..." James paused and fell silent, his mouth trembling and his eyes bright with tears, as his mother bade Catherine farewell and cheerfully left the chamber.

Sixteen

Catherine summoned Bess Holland as soon as Mistress Benson had departed, and introduced her protégé simply as James Benson.

"He will stay here at Kenninghall until his mother has given birth to her child," explained Catherine. "There is an unoccupied bedchamber on the other side of the passageway I believe."

"There is, my lady," nodded Bess Holland. "Shall I have it made ready for Master James?"

"Yes, it should do nicely and will enable me to keep an eye on him."

"I'll send a servant to transfer his clothes, my lady."

"Clothes?" Catherine looked doubtfully at the pathetically small bundle Mistress Benson had handed to her son before her departure.

"Yes, my clothes are in there," said the boy, following the direction of Catherine's gaze. "I'm wearing my Sunday best and mama tied the rest up in her old shawl."

Both women seemed lost for words as, unselfconsciously, he untied the shawl and displayed its shabby contents.

"Look, my lady, that's my everyday shirt and breeches, and –" His face lit up in surprise. "– so that was what mama was doing when she sat up late last night! See, my lady – she's made me a brand new shirt. It's even got lace round the collar and cuffs!"

"Where are your shoes and your hose?" asked Catherine.

"I've got them on," said the boy proudly, holding out each of his legs for inspection.

135

"Where are your others?" asked Catherine.

He looked surprised. "My others? Oh, I haven't got any others. I wear these for Sunday service and special occasions – like when I go to see His Lordship. The rest of the time I go barefooted like everyone else."

"Barefooted?" asked Catherine sternly, as if she suspected him of lying.

"Of course," said James in obvious amusement. "No one wears shoes all the time, now do they? It would be silly to wear them all the time, wouldn't it?"

"Why would it?" asked Catherine uncertainly.

"How would feet be able to grow if we wore shoes all the time?" asked the boy earnestly. "They'd never see the air and the rain and sunshine – and nothing grows without air and rain and sunshine."

"There speaks the country lad," laughed Catherine and turned to Bess. "Pray have one of the servants take Master James and his clothes to the bedchamber and show him where everything is, Mistress Holland."

As Bess departed, Catherine turned to James.

"'Twill be good to have you here, James," she said. "You remind me of my younger brother Richard. You would like Richard – he is the same age as you. It is nearing dinnertime and afterwards, if it is a fine afternoon, we might take a walk in the garden."

"And then I can see Richard, can't I, my lady?"

Catherine shook her head. "Alas, I fear that is not possible. Richard is at Sackville Hall, my home many miles from here," she told him, conscious of a sudden wave of homesickness.

James watched her in silence. "Never mind, my lady. I expect we'll see him one day," he said then, on a note of reassurance that touched Catherine's heart.

"I hope so, James," she said.

"Do you know His Lordship?"

"His Lordship?" asked Catherine in surprise. "To which gentleman are you referring?"

The boy looked puzzled. "Are there two gentlemen called that?" he asked.

"There are many gentlemen called so," Catherine told him.

"The His Lordship I mean is my father, you see, and when I visit him he gives me a gold piece and tells me to love mama and go with God."

"The His Lordship you mean, James, is indeed your father, but he is away in London at the present time," explained Catherine. "When he returns, you shall see him."

"Do you promise?"

"Of course."

"Does His Lordship do what you say, then?"

"Not necessarily," Catherine told him. "But His Lordship and I are of one mind on many things, and are shortly to be wed. We were betrothed when – Do you know what betrothed means, James?"

He shook his head. "Nay, my lady."

"It means that a man and woman have signed a document that makes them married in the sight of the law. But they are not truly married until they go to church and are married in the sight of God," explained Catherine. "His Lordship and I were betrothed when we were children."

"And you're going to be married in church when His Lordship returns, my lady, and then you'll be really and truly married."

"That is so, James."

The boy considered this for a few moments in silence.

"And then His Lordship will give me a gold piece and tell me to go home," he said then. "He'll tell me to love mama and to go with God."

"That could be how it will be." Catherine was suddenly and unaccountably tearful.

"Why are you crying?" the boy asked.

"I am not crying – not really. We must pray for them both, James."

"Both?"

"For His Lordship – and your mother," Catherine told him. "They have gone their separate ways and yet both of them, it seems to me, are greatly in need of our prayers. Please God no harm will come to either of them."

* * *

It was Bess Holland who brought Catherine the news next morning.

Catherine was still in bed, having slept badly, and was awakened at eight o'clock by Bess drawing back the curtains.

"Good morning, my lady," said Bess.

"Is something wrong, Mistress Holland?" asked Catherine, hurriedly sitting up in bed.

"Wrong, my lady?"

"It is unusual to see you so early in the day."

"I always rise early, my lady – old habits die hard, I suppose. But I mostly remain in my chamber till ten o'clock – the servants come to me there for their orders."

"Then something is wrong. Is there news of the Duke, or the Earl of Surrey?" Catherine hesitated. "Or of Lord Thomas perchance?"

"Nay, there's no news from London." Bess's voice expressed indifference. "The news I have is nearer home and will doubtless be of some concern to Master James. One of the sheriff's officers was here an hour ago enquiring about him, but when I told him the boy was safe, having been placed in your care by his mother yesterday, he seemed satisfied and went away."

"It concerns Master James, you say?" asked Catherine. "Then it must have to do with his mother, though the baby was not due for a further two weeks. Pray tell me what has happened, Mistress Holland."

"Mistress Benson is dead, alas."

"Dead?" asked Catherine incredulously. "Surely not! Please God you are mistaken!"

"It seems that Mistress Benson didn't tell anyone where she was going when she left home to come here with Master James yesterday," Bess explained. "By all accounts, she was scared out of her wits by that husband of hers."

"She told me that the cowman was keeping an eye on the other children in her absence," said Catherine.

"That was so, it seems, but when she hadn't returned to the farm by four o'clock in the afternoon, the cowman, concerned lest some ill had befallen her and Master James, informed Jake Benson of her absence."

"Four o'clock!" exclaimed Catherine in dismay. "But she must have left Kenninghall about eleven-thirty. She was anxious to get home before her husband returned for his dinner."

"When Farmer Benson learned that she and her son hadn't returned, he and some of the villagers organized a search for them."

"And?"

"It didn't take them long to find her – she was only a few minutes' walk from the farm. Her pains must have started when she was on her way home and she'd apparently stopped to rest by the side of the footpath, hoping to gain strength to resume her journey."

"Poor soul!" exclaimed Catherine. "If only she had accepted my offer of help!"

"Poor soul is right, my lady," agreed Bess grimly. "When they found her, she'd given birth there by the wayside. The child was apparently healthy, and she'd managed to sever the cord with her teeth and remove her own shawl to wrap him in."

"It was bitterly cold yesterday," observed Catherine. "Without her shawl and in a weakened condition, she must have been chilled to the marrow."

"When the search party found her, she'd been dead for several hours, 'tis thought – she'd died of haemorrhage and exposure to the cold."

"Mother of pity!" exclaimed Catherine aghast. "What of the child?"

"He was dead, but only just, it seems," said Bess. "She was holding him protectively in her arms when they found them – they had to prise her arms apart to release the child. He was still warm, but it was too late to revive him – just as well, if you ask me, for the poor motherless brat!"

"Motherless ..." Catherine said in dismay, as the full implication of the news dawned on her. "Our Lady have pity! Poor James! He too is motherless and it will be up to me to break the news to him. He was devoted to his mother and this will be a cruel blow, I fear."

"To think that his mother brought him here yesterday – in the nick of time as it were!" Bess said, thoughtfully. "It seems strange that she should bring her bastard to you."

"How do you know he is a bastard?" demanded Catherine.

"Everyone in the village knows it, my lady," Bess told her. "No one knows for sure who the boy's father is, but there are plenty of rumours needless to say. I've even heard it said that ..."

"I must ring for Lucy and get dressed immediately," Catherine interposed firmly, getting out of bed. "Then I shall have to go and tell James the news."

"Lucy is waiting in the ante-chamber, my lady," Bess told her. "I summoned her before I came in."

"Thank you, Mistress Holland," Catherine said absently, and turned a troubled gaze on the housekeeper. "Drusilla Benson must have had a premonition. She feared she would not survive the birth of the baby and – since her husband had no liking for the boy – I agreed to take charge of James, at least temporarily."

"Temporarily, my lady? Until Lord Thomas returns, do you mean?" asked Bess pointedly.

"Of course." Catherine's tone was deliberately casual. "As Lord Thomas is my affianced husband, I naturally wish to consult him before taking Master James permanently into my care."

* * *

James received the news of his mother's tragic death in silence. His face drained of colour, his life force seeming suddenly to be centred in his eyes, as he contemplated Catherine and the information she had given him.

"I am so sorry, James." Catherine, seated on the edge of his bed, was conscious of the inadequacy of words. "You loved your mother dearly I know."

Still the boy said nothing.

"You must not concern yourself about the future," Catherine went on. "That will be taken care of, I promise you."

"My stepfather ..." James paused.

"I have sent a message to your stepfather, telling him that you are in my care here at Kenninghall where you were placed by your mother yesterday," Catherine told him.

"My stepfather killed mama," said James. "She told him she wasn't to have another baby, but he gave her one just the same."

"You must not say that, James." Catherine said gently. "Only God can give babies."

"I wish you'd told mama that – she always blamed my stepfather." James said earnestly. "Anyway, it was all my fault."

"What was your fault?"

"Mama having another baby. Stepfather only let God give it to her because he was angry about me."

"Nonsense, James. Your mother died by misadventure," insisted Catherine. "It was nobody's fault. The baby was born early when your mother was out of doors and there was no one at hand to assist her. You must not blame yourself."

"Love your mother and go with God – that's what His Lordship always said to me. I *did* love her and I should have gone with God. If I'd run away – for good, like I meant to –" James burst into tears. "– then – stepfather – would – have – stopped – being – angry – because – of – me – and – he'd – have – stopped – God – from – giving – her – another – baby – and – she – wouldn't – have – brought – me – here – yesterday – to – make – stepfather – stop – beating – her ..."

Punctuated by sobs, his speech became incoherent at that point, and Catherine spoke firmly.

"Hearken to me, James," she said, her own eyes bright with tears. "You are upset and you know not what you are saying. I am going to ring for a servant now to bring you some hot milk and then I shall put a few drops of something special into it, and that will send you to sleep. When you have had a good rest and feel calmer, we will talk some more."

"There is no one to love me now, is there?" he said as he sipped the milk, shuddering at the slightly bitter taste.

"I love you, James," Catherine said gently.

"But you're a fine lady. You couldn't really love me – not like mama did. Besides, you're young and mama was quite old. I wish His Lordship was here now. If I go with God, do you think he would help me find His Lordship?"

"Methinks that already God has helped you to find His Lordship," Catherine said quietly. "He has sent you here to me, and that was the first step towards finding your father."

"And will he love me?"

"He loves you already, James," Catherine assured him as she tucked the bedclothes around him. "Try to sleep now."

"I wish mama could have seen His Lordship ..."

He fell asleep at that point, and Catherine remained by his bedside for a long time. Tears lay like morning dew upon his cheeks and in sleep he looked younger than his seven years.

He looks defenceless and very vulnerable, Catherine thought to herself. Already his arrival here has given warmth and new purpose to my life here at Kenninghall. How strange that is! Had I known beforehand of his arrival, I would have viewed it with dismay. How can I live under the same roof as my lord's bastard? I would have said to myself.

Perchance it is all part of a plan. Already I have a great fondness for the child, and his presence here is curiously comforting. It seems to me that the lives of both of us are close-linked with Thomas Howard and that, in my lord's absence, James brings him closer to me. Oh how I long to see my lord and tell him of his beloved bastard!

Seventeen

Mary summoned Bess Holland to her apartment next morning. For a long time they sat together in the living-chamber, discussing Mary's audience with the King and its repercussions.

"It seems you accomplished your purpose admirably, my lady," smiled Bess, as Mary told her what had befallen.

"That remains to be seen," sighed Mary. "It could well be that both my father and Henry will be let off with a caution. His Majesty paid little heed to my evidence – he poured scorn on the idea of Henry having committed treason. Although they have been sent to the Tower, it seems likely that there is insufficient evidence to bring either of them to justice."

"To justice?" asked Bess. "You speak as if you yourself actually believe them guilty of treason."

"I most certainly do believe it," insisted Mary. "Think you I would have acted thus, against my own flesh and blood, without good cause?"

"Oh, you had good cause, my lady," admitted Bess. "There's no denying that. We both had good cause, did we not? We saw the destruction of your father and brother as the means to a better life."

"Do not speak thus!" Mary's face was ashen. "Could I live with myself if I had acted so from selfish motives? Do not dare speak thus or ... "

"Or what, my lady?" interposed Bess quietly. "Would you complain of me to your lord father? Would you have me dismissed from the household? Nay, 'tis a bit late for that. You've acted in your best interests – and mine – and soon you will reap your reward."

"My reward?" asked Mary curiously. "Tom Seymour, do you mean?"

"Of course," nodded Bess. "Why else did you seek audience with His Majesty?"

"Tom Seymour will never be mine – I realize that now," Mary said slowly. "Henry was right in his assessment of him. He is a time-serving opportunist of the worst kind – methinks I always knew that!"

"Yet you still love him," Bess said matter-of-factly.

"Yet I still love him and, Heaven help me, shall continue so to do."

"You talked with him while you were at Court? Is that the reason for your despondency?"

"I talked with him and it was then I learned the truth," Mary said ruefully. "That is why I say he will never be mine."

"He does not love you?"

"Love me!" Mary laughed mirthlessly. "Tom Seymour loves no one but himself. Tom Seymour is an ambitious man. Oh, he was honest enough with me – too honest for my peace of mind. What had he to lose, after all? I could hardly go to the King and inform him of Tom Seymour's traitorous utterances, only a few hours after I had informed him of the traitorous utterances of Tom Seymour's enemy, my own brother!"

"What did Tom Seymour say to you?" asked Bess curiously.

"He spoke of the succession. He said: 'When the King dies, he will leave a widow, one son and two daughters.' " Mary spoke as if she had many times mulled the words over in her mind and they came readily to her lips. " 'His son will be proclaimed King and, as the new King's uncle, my brother will become Lord Protector and rule in his name, while I shall marry the widow, Katherine Parr, and thereby become guardian of the two princesses.' "

"And what did you say to that, my lady?" asked Bess. "Didn't you remind him of his promise to marry you once the chief obstacles, your father and brother, were out of the way?"

"Oh, I reminded him – though I should have known

better," Mary said bitterly. "Already I guessed what his answer would be, but I had to be sure – ever since, I squirm with humiliation whenever I am reminded of it!"

"Pray tell me his answer, my lady," Bess said sympathetically. "You know you can trust me not to speak of it to anyone else."

Mary's eyes brimmed with tears of self-pity. "His answer was short and to the point. He said: 'Since it would appear that the power of the Howards is – to say the least – in the descendancy, what would it profit Tom Seymour to wed the Duke of Norfolk's daughter?'"

So, thought Bess, my lady Mary is hoist with her own petard! By weakening, if not destroying, the power of the Duke, she has lowered her value in the marriage market. Well, I'm not likely to lose any sleep over that! She's a selfish hussy, that one, and always was. She's her mother's child and, as such, would be a bundle of trouble for any man fool enough to marry her.

But what of myself? How does the matter affect me? If the Duke is ruined, and Her Ladyship has mismanaged the fine match that was to have done us both a bit of good, where does that leave me? Perchance I should cut my losses while there is yet time. There are guards at each exit, it is true, but dressed up as the laundry-maid I once was, doubtless I'd by-pass them without much ado.

As soon as I see my opportunity, I shall be off. I shall collect up my jewellery – it must be worth a fortune – and pack it into a laundry basket with a few of my best gowns. Most of my fine clothes will have to be left behind, alas – but you can't have everything in this life!

"Tom Seymour sounds a very unpleasant fellow, my lady," she said to Mary. "'Tis a good thing you saw him in his true colours before it was too late – you're well rid of him, if you ask me!"

"Is it too late?" asked Mary. "Even now I would marry him if I had the chance. Alas, that I did not leave the matter to take its course – then at least I should have kept my illusions! Had I refused to hearken to your persuasions … "

Mary stopped in mid-sentence as she heard a peremptory knock on her door. Before she could answer, the door was flung open and a man strode into the chamber.

Mary stood up and confronted the intruder.

"Who in God's name are you, sir?" she asked angrily.

"Sir Richard Southwell at your service, my lady," came the answer.

"By the Mass!" exclaimed Mary. "But you are friend to my brother, the Earl of Surrey!"

"A slight correction, my lady," Southwell said evenly. "I was friend to the Earl of Surrey."

"Then since you are, by your own admission, no longer my brother's friend, pray tell me what brings you here," Mary said haughtily. "And in so unmannerly a fashion."

"As former friend to Surrey ... "

"You have turned informer," interposed Mary in sudden realization. "That is the truth, is it not?"

"'Tis the duty of all His Majesty's subjects to inform His Majesty and the Privy Council when danger threatens His Majesty's crown and dignity," said Southwell piously. "You, by your own recent example, my lady, have given us the lead in that."

"Again I ask: why are you here, sir? Answer me immediately or I shall summon the guards."

"That would avail you nothing, my lady. The guards take their orders from me," Southwell told her. "But I shall none the less acquaint you with the reason for my being here. The Privy Council has selected myself and two assistants, who are at present waiting outside this chamber, to seek further evidence against the Earl of Surrey. We have reason to believe that you yourself, my lady, can assist us in this matter, and we also wish to question a certain Mistress Holland, said to be the housekeeper here."

"I am Mistress Holland," Bess told him. "I shall be happy to assist you with your enquiries, though naturally as a mere housekeeper ... "

Bess allowed her modest words to fade into silence.

"I must make it clear, sir," said Mary, "that I abhor your

presence here. As my brother's friend, you would have been welcome. As his enemy, your presence is an intrusion. Ask your questions therefore, if you must, and then be on your way."

"Thanks in part to you, my lady, the Duke your father and the Earl your brother have been arrested and are now lodged in the Tower," Southwell reminded her. "You have already laid certain information against them and can, I trust, give us more."

Mary calmly reseated herself and appeared to be giving consideration to the matter, while Southwell went to the door and summoned his assistants.

"Pray pardon this added intrusion, my lady," Southwell said. "It is necessary that these gentlemen should be present, that they may act as witnesses."

What have I to lose? Mary was thinking. I hate my father and Henry – but for them, I would long ago have become a contented wife and mother. Even now it might not be too late. Once the power of my father and Henry is destroyed, I could plead with His Majesty, my father-in-law, to provide me with a suitable husband.

Perchance even now Tom Seymour could be mine. He prated of his own schemes and ambitions – but what if the King is not as ill as is suggested? His Majesty is in his fifty-sixth year and could well have many years ahead of him. What then? Tom Seymour makes pretence of scorning my regard for him, but I am not deceived. He takes a delight in taunting and humiliating me, but that is his nature. There was a time when he wanted me for myself, rather than for ambition's sake. As none knows better than I, that which Tom Seymour wants he takes …

She looked steadily at Southwell.

"Though I love my father, and my brother whom I know to be a rash gentleman, yet will I conceal nothing," she said. "My duty to the King, my father-in-law, must take precedence over all other considerations."

"Your loyalty does you credit, my lady," Southwell said ambiguously. "Pray speak freely in answer to my questions.

Do not be afraid. Honesty, like loyalty, brings its own reward."

"I will do my best, sir."

"Has your brother, to your knowledge, ever acted against the interests of the King?"

"He had a portrait of himself inscribed with the mottoes *Sat Superest* and *Tel Dandus,*" Mary told him. "It seemed to me that this was a threat to His Majesty's heirs."

"Was the Duke your father acquainted with this portrait, my lady?"

Mary seemed to hesitate. "He was aware of it," she said, as if with reluctance.

"Did he express disapproval?"

"Nay, he praised the portrait," lied Mary, "and expressed himself well pleased with the mottoes."

"Do you know of any other way in which your brother acted contrary to His Majesty's interests, my lady?" asked Southwell. "I regret the necessity for asking you of such matters, and do so only out of concern for His Majesty's well-being."

"My brother warned me against individual interpretation of the Scriptures, for he himself is a professed Papist," Mary said, with truth this time. "He went so far as to accuse me of Lutheran leanings, and suggested I had allowed myself to be influenced by Mistress Holland."

Southwell turned to look consideringly at Bess, but then he again turned his attention to Mary.

"Your brother's accusations were untrue, my lady?" he asked.

"Of course," declared Mary indignantly. "Would I, daughter-in-law to His Majesty and daughter to England's premier duke, hearken to the maunderings of a servant?"

"It is a comparatively trivial matter, my lady," Southwell pointed out. "As you may be aware, His Majesty abhors Lutheran teachings and still favours Catholic dogma and forms of worship. Have you any further information?"

"I think not, sir," said Mary, still a trifle on her mettle.

"It is my duty to remind you that there are severe penalties for withholding information in matters of treason."

"There is one other thing … " Mary paused tantalisingly.

"Pray continue, my lady."

"It is a somewhat delicate matter, sir."

"I would hear of it none the less."

"I am loth to speak of it but, in view of your reminder of the penalties for withholding information, it would seem I have little choice."

"Pray continue."

"My brother suggested that I – that I ... " Mary modestly lowered her gaze and tried again. "He suggested that I should become the King's mistress."

"God's life!" exclaimed Southwell, looking suitably shocked. "What was your brother's purpose in making such a suggestion?"

"He said that if I became the King's mistress, I could then use my influence to buy favours for my family and himself." Mary's expression was one of outraged modesty. "He said I should follow the example of Madame d'Estampes, who is mistress to the King of France."

"Jesu! And to think I once called Surrey friend!" exclaimed Southwell. "Could it be that you misunderstood his meaning, my lady?"

"I fear not, sir," said Mary sadly. "I fear not. Would that I could answer you differently!"

"Is it just possible that the Earl your brother was jesting?" asked Southwell.

Mary shook her head. "Nay, he meant every word he said, alas. When I remonstrated with him, for I was deeply shocked by the suggestion, my brother became angry and abusive. He has, as you surely know, a hasty temper."

"That any gentleman could seek to use his sister for such purpose is beyond belief!" declared Southwell. "Nevertheless, I can see, from your understandable reluctance to speak of the matter, that you are telling the truth."

"But for my loyalty to His Majesty, I would not have spoken of it at any cost," Mary said sanctimoniously. "One does one's duty, but it is a sad business – a very sad business!"

"I am grateful to you for your frankness, my lady," Southwell told her. "Your information could be most valuable in bringing a criminal to justice. I need detain you no longer. I have yet to interrogate Mistress Holland, and then my men and I will return post-haste to Westminster.''

"This is indeed a sad day for you and me, Sir Richard," Mary said with a wan smile. "You, my brother's erstwhile friend, and I, his sister, have both been called to a loathsome duty.''

"For King and country, my lady," Southwell reminded her. "We have done our duty for King and country!''

He turned to Bess who had listened to the bizarre exchange in silence, while not troubling to conceal a sardonic smile.

"Now, Mistress Holland, kindly step into the adjoining chamber," he said briskly. "I have a few questions for you also.''

* * *

As Bess preceded him into the adjoining chamber, Southwell indicated to his assistants that they were to remain outside the door.

"Pray be seated, Mistress Holland," he said pleasantly. "You are housekeeper here at Kenninghall, I understand.''

"That is so, sir," nodded Bess.

"And for how long have you occupied your position?" asked Southwell.

"Twenty-seven years, sir.''

"Twenty-seven years? You surprise me, Mistress Holland. After so long in the Duke's employ, you must be well acquainted with the Howard family.''

"I do my duty, sir," Bess said primly.

Southwell looked her up and down, not troubling to conceal his interest. He saw the expensive gown, the jewelled rings and necklaces, the french hood lavishly trimmed with pearls – and the voluptuous figure and bold gaze.

"You are said to be the Duke of Norfolk's mistress," he said.

"I am said to be a great many things," shrugged Bess. "Some are true – some are not.''

"Then you deny it?''

"I did not say that – pray do not put words into my mouth, sir."

"According to the Duchess of Norfolk, you have been her husband's mistress these twenty-seven years past," said Southwell.

"Then it must be so," said Bess carelessly. "Who am I to disagree with a duchess?"

"You admit your fault?"

"My fault?" Bess laughed huskily. "I am, as you said, in the Duke's employ. He is master of Kenninghall – and a master chooses his own mistress. Could I have refused to warm the Duke's bed – even had I so wished?"

"You seem like a woman who knows her own mind." Southwell's emphasis on the word 'woman' was not lost on Bess. "Did not you resent the situation?"

"What if I did?" asked Bess. "I have been well paid for my services."

"You own a valuable collection of jewels, I understand. Naturally you wish to keep them."

"Naturally," agreed Bess.

"Then I suggest you tell me everything you know about the Duke your master."

"Everything? Fie, sir! Modesty forbids me to tell you everything!"

Southwell seemed suddenly angry. "Enough of this play-acting, Mistress Holland. If you refuse to answer my questions, I shall summon my assistants. You will be stripped and searched and any jewellery found on you will be – er – confiscated."

"Confiscated?" repeated Bess coolly. "To confiscate, I have always understood, means to seize by authority. Kindly tell me, sir, by whose authority my jewellery would be removed?"

"By the authority vested in me by the Privy Council," Southwell answered – just as coolly. "It is only fair to warn you that my men are not renowned for gallantry or gentleness – and after they had searched you, your chamber also would be searched."

"And if I answer your questions – what then?" asked Bess.

"Will my valuables still be confiscated?"

"Tell me all you know of the Duke's political intrigues and ambitions, and you will not be molested," Southwell told her.

"I am the Duke's mistress – not his confidante! Why would he tell me his secrets?"

"Why? I will tell you why, Mistress Holland," sneered Southwell, "Just as, it is said, every man has his price – so, it could also be said, every man needs a confidante. From information we have received, it would seem that you have filled that office admirably."

"And if I tell you what you wish to know, I shall be permitted to keep my jewellery?"

"Of course."

Bess sighed. "Then you leave me no choice, sir. I will tell you all," she said.

"I want the truth, mind," insisted Southwell. "Once I have your information, I shall return to London. Should it subsequently be discovered that you have lied or withheld any relevant matter, I promise you I shall be back."

"I can scarcely wait!" Bess said, mockingly.

"Should I return, you would rue the day," warned Southwell. "I should see to it that you were taken before the justices at Norwich and charged with being a common whore."

"But … "

"You know what that would mean, do you not? I see by your expression that you do – you would have more than the loss of your jewellery to concern you then! You'd be sentenced to be whipped naked at a cart's tail – and a whore who's been punished thus is never a pretty sight!"

"I will tell you all I know," Bess said then. "Though there's little enough I can add to what the Duchess of Richmond's already told you."

"We need more than that if we are to see justice done to that old reprobate," Southwell told her. "So, if you value your good looks, Mistress Holland, you had better think of a few embellishments to add to your story."

"I shall do my best, sir."

What does it matter anyway? Bess thought to herself. So long as what I say will satisfy this obnoxious creature and send him back to Westminster post-haste, it matters not what tale I concoct. As soon as he's gone, I shall make my escape just as I'd planned – and then it will take a cleverer man than Richard Southwell to discover Bess Holland's whereabouts!

"I feel sure you will, Mistress Holland," Southwell was saying. "And to make it easy for you, I shall ask the questions, and you will answer simply 'yea' or 'nay.' That should save us both time and trouble."

Eighteen

Kenninghall had become a confused and unhappy household.

Alarmed by the visit of Southwell and his men, and having learned from Lucy of the interrogation of Mary and Bess Holland, Catherine, accompanied by James, remained in her own apartment.

Gossip and speculation were rife in the household. Mary had refused to see anyone since Southwell's departure, and the sound of weeping, it was said, was heard frequently coming from her apartment.

Bess Holland had fled the house, leaving the running of the household to one of the upper servants. When her absence had first been noticed and reported to Mary, an inspection of her chamber had revealed that her jewellery too was missing.

The guards' captain having been informed of Bess's disappearance, it then came to light that, carrying a laundry basket and disguised as a laundry-maid, and ostensibly bound for the wash-house outside, she had hoodwinked one of the guards into letting her pass.

A deep bond of affection had grown up between Catherine and James. Eager to please and to learn, James had quickly adapted to the ways of the nobility, while Catherine took pleasure in teaching him the rudiments of reading and writing, of speaking and conducting himself correctly, and in giving instructions to the sewing-maids for the making of new clothes for him. She had told him of his father, explaining who he was, and telling him that she and his father were soon to be married.

She taught him some of the games she had played in her

not-far-distant childhood, and joined whole-heartedly in those he had formerly played with his half-brothers and half-sisters. During the hour that preceded his bedtime, sounds of merriment were frequently heard coming from Catherine's chamber where, joined by Lucy, Catherine forgot her own anxieties for a time in taking part in the lively games of a seven-year-old.

It was plain that James had taken readily to his new mode of life, and for much of the time he seemed happy and carefree. But sometimes he would creep away unobserved and Catherine would discover him later in his chamber weeping distractedly for his mother. She comforted him then as best she could, assuring him of her love and protection, and telling him that his father's return would not be delayed much longer.

"When you marry His Lordship, you will be my stepmother, will you not?" he asked her on one such occasion.

"I shall indeed," smiled Catherine.

"Then I shall have a father and a stepmother, instead of a mother and a stepfather," James said soberly. "Perchance His Lordship won't want me to live here."

"Of course he will want you here," Catherine assured him.

"How do you know he will? You haven't asked him."

"I do not need to ask him. I know he loves you, for he told me so, and I know he will want you here if I do."

"And do you, my lady?" he asked, the anxiety in his voice tugging at her heart-strings.

"I do," she said softly. "I want the three of us to be together more than anything else in the world."

* * *

On the third day after Southwell's visit, Catherine sat alone by the fire in brooding melancholy, affected by the gloom that had settled over most of the household.

James was in his bedchamber, absorbed in playing with some wooden toy soldiers that had once belonged to his father, and which he and Catherine had discovered in one of the disused nurseries that morning.

It was approaching dusk, and the candles remained unlit by Catherine's order. It seemed to her that the misty gloom of a December twilight accorded well with her own dejection, her increasing sense of unease and impending disaster.

Almost three weeks had passed since Lord Thomas's departure, and yet still Catherine had received no communication from him. Puzzled and not a little alarmed by his inexplicable silence, she nevertheless had no choice than to remain where she was and hope that news – or better still, Lord Thomas himself – was on the way.

The door was suddenly opened, startling Catherine from her thoughts, and Lucy hurried unceremoniously into the chamber. It was at once apparent to Catherine that her maid had some news to impart.

"There's a messenger just arrived in the courtyard, my lady," Lucy said breathlessly. "He's dusty and travel-stained from hard riding and he's accompanied by men-at-arms."

"Do you know whence he comes?" asked Catherine anxiously.

"He's wearing the Sackville livery, one of the grooms told me, my lady. He's in a great hurry, it seems. He gave orders to his men to see to the horses and seek refreshment for themselves, and then he strode into the entrance hall and insisted on seeing Your Ladyship immediately."

"My lord father must have sent him," said Catherine. "Pray hurry and show him in, Lucy – the poor man is probably nigh to dropping with weariness!"

As the girl disappeared, Catherine waited impatiently. *Why has father sent a messenger here now, and in such haste? Has someone been taken ill? Or died perchance? Father must have some urgent news to impart to me ...*

"Fowler!" she exclaimed then as Lucy ushered in the messenger. "What brings you to Kenninghall in such haste?"

"I bring you a letter from your lord father, my lady," replied the messenger. "He told me to say that he wishes you to read it at once, in my presence, and thereafter give me your instructions."

"Pray be seated, Fowler," said Catherine as she took the

letter. "You must be weary from your journey."

"My orders were to hasten here with all speed, my lady," said the messenger, sinking gratefully into a chair.

Catherine turned to Lucy. "Send for refreshments for my father's messenger," she said, before breaking the seal of the letter and starting to read.

The letter was brief and to the point:

"Earl of Dorset to Lady Catherine Sackville."

"My dear daughter,

"Time is short so I must needs be brief: already my men are mounted up ready for departure.

"I command you, on your duty as my daughter, to leave Kenninghall forthwith, and return, escorted by my men-at-arms, here to Sackville.

"I suggest that, if she be willing, your personal maid accompanies you on your journey, which could well be fraught with discomfort at this time of the year.

"On your arrival here, I will acquaint you with the reasons for this my command. Suffice it to say in the meantime that I fear for your safety at Kenninghall.

"Your most affectionate loving father
"Dorset"

*"Written this sixteenth day
of December 1546
at Sackville Hall."*

Watching Catherine as she read the letter, Lucy registered her mistress's trembling hands and sudden pallor.

"Best be seated, my lady," she said. "You look a trifle unwell. I trust you've not received bad news."

"My father commands me to return to Sackville forthwith," Catherine told her, letting Lucy assist her to a chair. "He says little else."

"Return to Sackville?" said Lucy in dismay. "But why, my lady?"

"I know not. My father's letter was written in haste and he says he will explain the reason for his command on my arrival."

"But, my lady, what if Lord Thomas should return and you are no longer here?"

"Then he will learn that I have returned to Sackville," said Catherine. "My father would not have commanded my return, except for some very good reason."

"But, my lady …"

"He suggests that you accompany me," interposed Catherine. "What do you say to that, Lucy?"

Lucy gazed at her in silence for a few moments.

"I don't know, I'm sure, my lady," she said at length. "I'm in the Howard family's employ, and anyway I'd not want to leave Norfolk for good – all my folks dwell nearby, as you know, and I've never been further than Norwich in my life."

"Then you will not come with me?"

Suddenly Lucy smiled. "I'll come with you, my lady. I'd not be sorry to leave Kenninghall for a while – all the comings and goings of the past weeks have fair given me the creeps!"

"Then that is settled," said Catherine, who had taken a liking to the girl. "You shall come with me to Sackville. But I promise you that, whatever the outcome of the present situation, I myself shall see to it that you eventually return to Norfolk – should you still wish it."

"What of Master James, my lady?"

"He too will be going with me."

"I'd best get busy right away then with packing your clothes and Master James's, my lady," Lucy said, already making towards Catherine's clothes closet. "Now I'm getting used to the idea, I can see it will be quite an adventure! Fancy me taking a journey to foreign parts!"

"How soon should we be ready to leave, Fowler?" Catherine asked the messenger.

"'Tis almost dark, my lady, and my men and horses need a night's rest," he answered. "I suggest we start out just before daybreak on the morrow. There are few hours of daylight at this time of year and I'd like to be well on our way by tomorrow night – lest the weather breaks and we're beset by snow."

"We shall be ready," Catherine assured him.

Nineteen

Catherine received a rapturous welcome from her family when, after a long and exhausting journey, she arrived at Sackville Hall.

Snow had fallen overnight but, warned of her approach by the look-out on the battlements, Lord Dorset, his sons Edward and Richard, and his daughters, Cecily, Margaret and Anne, were all there in the courtyard to greet her.

There were cries of excitement and joy, smiles and hugs and questions – and even a few tears. James was introduced to the family and was at once taken charge of by Catherine's brother Richard, the youngest member of the family, who was delighted at the prospect of a new playmate.

As she was escorted into the house by her chattering sisters, Catherine was able for a while to set aside her anxiety over the reason for her return. She savoured the pleasure of being home once more among the familiar faces and surroundings of her childhood.

"Take Catherine and her maidservant to her bedchamber," Lord Dorset said firmly to his other daughters, "and then leave them alone for a while to recover from the rigours of their journey."

"But, papa, we have not seen Catherine for ages," protested Margaret.

"And we have so many questions to ask her," put in Cecily.

"None that cannot wait," said Lord Dorset.

"We have been longing to hear about Kenninghall and Catherine's betrothed," pouted Anne, the youngest sister. "Please papa, dearest papa, let us …"

Lord Dorset shook his head. "There will be plenty of opportunity for all that later, so kindly do as I say. As soon as you have had time to remove the dust of your journey and don fresh clothes, Catherine, the servants shall bring refreshments to your chamber."

"Thank you, papa," smiled Catherine. "In truth, I am not at all weary now. I felt dreadfully tired this morning but, now that I am here, my tiredness has quite disappeared."

"In that case, papa ..." Margaret started to say.

Lord Dorset interposed. "Indeed I am glad to hear it, Catherine. All the same, you do need rest. You look pale, and you are thinner than when you left home. After you have partaken of food, have a good rest."

"I will do as you say, papa."

"I shall expect you in my library in two hours' time," Lord Dorset told her. "We have matters to discuss, my daughter."

Reminded of her fears, Catherine's smile faded. "I shall be there, papa," she nodded.

* * *

Catherine was quite unable to sleep during her siesta. Her body was refreshed and rested, but her mind was restless with apprehension.

What has father to tell me? she wondered. Pleased as he was at our reunion, I nevertheless sensed that he had something on his mind. Only some serious happening would have induced him to command my return. Perchance he has received news of the Duke, and has learned that the situation has taken a turn for the worse. Or could it be that, in the absence of the Duke and my lord Thomas, he disapproved of my remaining in a house ruled by Bess Holland? Could it be that father feared that I would be compromised, or in moral danger – he is very stern in such matters ...

Unable to bear the suspense any longer, she knocked on the library door a good ten minutes before the time arranged. She nevertheless received an immediate answer from her father.

Clearly he had been waiting for her, and was in no way

surprised by her early arrival. His smile, Catherine noted with relief, was cheerful enough as he bade her be seated opposite him by the fire.

"These past weeks cannot have been easy for you, my daughter," he said then. "Had I but an inkling of the catastrophic events which were so soon to follow on your arrival at Kenninghall, you would naturally not have gone to Norfolk."

"I have no regrets about going to Kenninghall, papa," Catherine assured him.

He looked searchingly at her. "You surprise me. In the letters you sent to your sisters and myself, you conveyed an impression of homesickness."

"Indeed I was homesick at first, papa, but of late everything had changed."

Lord Dorset smiled ruefully. "Such is surely an understatement, my daughter! Everything has indeed changed – both at Kenninghall itself and in the fortunes of the Howard family. And yet you speak as if the changes were to your liking – how could that be?"

"I was referring, father, to certain changes that took place prior to Viscount Bindon's departure from Kenninghall," explained Catherine. "Of course I still missed you all and it is wonderful to be here at Sackville again, but ..." Catherine hesitated.

"Tell me, my daughter."

"Only a few days before Viscount Bindon received the news of his brother's arrest, and departed forthwith for London, he and I formed a close attachment," Catherine said shyly. "I love him dearly, papa."

"Then it is as I thought."

"How so, papa?" asked Catherine in surprise. "You suggested just now that my letters to you conveyed only unhappiness."

"A messenger from Whitehall delivered a letter to me from Viscount Bindon," Lord Dorset explained. "His Lordship spoke of your mutual regard for each other – it was this regard that prompted him to write to me as he did, begging me to bring about your removal from Kenninghall with all speed."

"When did you receive Lord Thomas's letter, papa?" asked Catherine.

"Lord Thomas?"

"Viscount Bindon – he is addressed as Lord Thomas at Kenninghall," explained Catherine.

"I received the letter on 16th December – the same day that Fowler set forth with my letter to you," Lord Dorset told her. "I lost no time in acting on Lord Thomas's advice."

"I do not understand, papa. When my lord departed from Kenninghall, he expected to be away no more than two weeks. He told me of the dangers that threatened his father and brother, and of his reason for going to London." Catherine was unable to keep the tell-tale tremor from her voice. "Since his departure, I have received no communication from him – and yet you tell me he has written to you."

"He feared that any letters sent to Kenninghall would be intercepted – as is undoubtedly the case," Lord Dorset explained. "He was concerned lest you be implicated in the possible downfall of his family, and he wished at all costs to protect you from involvement."

"Then the situation has worsened?" asked Catherine. "Or could it be that my lord kept the full seriousness of the matter from me?"

Lord Dorset's voice was carefully controlled. "The Earl of Surrey's trial has taken place at the Guildhall. He conducted his own defence for, as you may know, the defendant is not allowed the benefit of counsel when charged with high treason. For eight hours, Surrey remained in the dock, arguing and reasoning – but to little purpose."

"Why so, papa?"

"His enemies, it would seem, had done their work well. Their scruples overcome by the Seymour gold that lined their pockets – even one of Surrey's closest friends, Sir Richard Southwell, gave evidence against him! – witnesses perjured themselves to bear false evidence."

Lord Dorset paused, as if what he had to say were not to his liking and he was selecting his words with care.

"Tell me, papa," pleaded Catherine. "Tell me the outcome –

keep me not in suspense!''

"The jury retired to consider the verdict, and a further six hours elapsed before they returned and pronounced the prisoner guilty.''

"Guilty!'' exclaimed Catherine. "But guilty of what, papa?''

"Guilty of high treason against, as it was expressed, 'the King's Majesty, his crown and dignity.' ''

"And?''

"Surrey was sentenced to death.'' Lord Dorset's voice was unemotional, and belied his own disquiet. "He is to be beheaded on 20th January on Tower Hill.''

"Mother of mercy!'' exclaimed Catherine aghast. "I had no idea it would come to this. Surrey has always been greatly favoured by the King, and I cannot believe him guilty of high treason. His Majesty will reprieve him, will he not?''

"A year ago – even six months ago – I would have had no doubt of it.'' Lord Dorset sighed. "Now, who can tell?''

"But what is different now, papa?''

"The King, though in only his fifty-sixth year, is in failing health, my daughter. His only son, Edward, is an ailing child of some ten summers. It is therefore likely that His Majesty fears that, in the event of his own death, the Howards will seize power. The Seymour brothers – who have sought unceasingly to destroy the Howards – are Edward's uncles and will have his best interests at heart: so, rightly or wrongly, reasons His Majesty. His love for his son and his hopes for the future of the House of Tudor, outweigh any other considerations – even his affection for Surrey.''

"Then there is scant hope of a reprieve, papa?'' asked Catherine.

"I know not, my daughter,'' admitted Lord Dorset. "I know not and that is the truth. Please God, the King will be merciful!''

"I can scarcely believe it, papa. Surrey is so gallant and full of life. He just cannot die – not now, like that! And what of Lady Frances? She and Surrey are devoted to each other – he is her whole life! Alas, that I did not remain in Norfolk after all.''

"Why speak you thus, Catherine?" asked Lord Dorset sternly.

"Maybe my presence would have been some small comfort to Frances." Catherine's eyes were bright with tears. "We had become such good friends."

"In the event of Surrey's death, his Countess will be placed under the protection of her father, the Earl of Oxford," Lord Dorset told her. "It would have been unwise for you to involve yourself at such a time."

"But Frances is my friend, papa," Catherine said reproachfully. "She is with child, and has asked me to be one of the baby's godmothers. The birth is expected in – in ... Sweet Jesus have pity! The child could well be born just three weeks after its father's death!"

"You must not distress yourself ..."

"How else could I feel?" put in Catherine. "Think you, if I had known the outcome of Surrey's trial, I would have deserted Frances at such a time?"

"I know you would not have done so, my daughter, and I suspect that Lord Thomas knows it also and was anxious therefore to prevent your being involved," Lord Dorset said quietly. "That was one of the reasons why, in commanding your return from Kenninghall, I did not furnish you with the facts."

"You say that was one of the reasons, papa," remarked Catherine. "Was there some other reason also?"

Lord Dorset seemed not to have heard the question.

"I understand your compassion for Lady Frances and I commend you for it," he said. "But one must be practical."

"How so, papa?"

"One must leave her to the care of those who have the power to help her – and must give thought to one's own sorrow."

"But Frances's sorrow is my sorrow also, papa."

"You fail to understand, Catherine," her father said gravely. "I was not referring then to Lady Frances."

But Catherine was looking at him warily, as if suddenly she had recognised his meaning.

" 'One must give thought to one's own sorrow' – that was

what you said, papa," she said slowly. "Then ..."

She fell silent, and Lord Dorset watched her expression, her dawning awareness of sorrow as yet unrealized.

"There is something else, is there not?" she asked softly. "There is something you have not told me. I registered the fact that you did not show me my lord's letter to you, that I myself might read it."

"There is more," admitted Lord Dorset, gazing down at the letter he was holding in his hand. "The Duke of Norfolk was sent for trial two days after Surrey."

"And?"

"He was convicted of high treason and sentenced to be executed on 27th January."

"May the saints protect us!" exclaimed Catherine. "So Mary has achieved her design."

"Mary?"

"The Duchess of Richmond," explained Catherine. "She went to the King with evidence concocted by the Duke's mistress, Bess Holland, and herself. Alas, papa, is it not too dreadful! If the Duke and Surrey are executed, Mary will have committed patricide and fratricide."

"Perchance you have been misinformed, Catherine. Doubtless Kenninghall has been a hot-bed of gossip and false rumour during the past weeks!"

"It is true enough, alas," sighed Catherine. "My lord Thomas told me, before he left Kenninghall, of his sister's treachery. Would that I could believe otherwise! When you have lived with people and got to know them, a happening such as this is like a nightmare."

"I understand your feelings, my daughter," Lord Dorset said gently. "I was not sure how much Lord Thomas had told you. There can be no doubt, alas, that the Duchess of Richmond contributed towards the downfall of her father and brothers – but it took minds far more cunning and devious than hers, I fancy, to bring them to total disaster."

"You said 'brothers.'" Catherine gazed at her father in sudden horror. "You said 'brothers,' papa. I beg you tell me that it was no more than a slip of the tongue – that my lord

Thomas is not in danger."

"Would that I could offer you such assurance, my child!" declared Lord Dorset. "Alas, I cannot. That is why I did not show you His Lordship's letter. I wished to break the news as gently as possible."

"Tell me, father," Catherine whispered.

"Thomas Howard, Viscount Bindon, was arrested and sent for trial the day after his father the Duke," Lord Dorset said formally. "He was charged with conspiring with his father and brother to commit high treason."

"And the verdict?" asked Catherine, seeing her father's hesitation. "What of the verdict?"

"He was found guilty as charged and was condemned to death," Lord Dorset told her. "He is to be beheaded on 27th January – the same day as his father."

Catherine was assailed by sudden faintness, and gripped the arms of her chair for support.

"It cannot be," she said, when the ringing in her ears had subsided. "It just cannot be. My Lord Thomas is innocent of the charge. He plays no part in political intrigues, and attends the Court only when duty demands it."

"He has none the less been convicted, my daughter."

"But why, papa?" cried Catherine. "Pray tell me why. He is no more guilty of treason than you and I – you believe that, do you not?"

"What you or I believe is of little relevance, Catherine," pointed out her father. "Even the truth, I fear, is of little relevance in this case. Those in high places believe what they want to believe, as often as not, and there are those who want to believe the Duke of Norfolk and his sons guilty of treason."

"But why, father?" Catherine asked again. "It is all so wicked and unfair. Why should my lord Thomas be treated thus?"

"He is a Howard," Lord Dorset said quietly. "That, dear child, is the simple answer. As such, during this time of uncertainty due to the King's ill-health, he is a potential danger to the House of Tudor. He is a Howard and, like ourselves, a Catholic – those facts are sufficient to cost him his life."

"Something must be done, my lord," Catherine said tremulously. "Could not you yourself go to His Majesty and plead for him?"

"Think you I have not considered such action already my daughter?" demanded Lord Dorset. "I sat up the whole of one night giving thought to it, seeking for ways and means of gaining Lord Thomas's release – I fear that the Duke and Surrey are more deeply involved – before rejecting the idea. I would be placing my own family in jeopardy – and for naught."

"Nay, papa, it would not be for naught," insisted Catherine. "It would be for the sake of justice. What if I myself were to go to His Majesty and beg for clemency, as his bride-to-be, for my lord Thomas?"

"In doing so, you would be acting contrary to Lord Thomas's wishes," Lord Dorset said quietly.

"How so?"

"He was adamant on that matter, my daughter. He begged me, in his letter, to see to it that you were in no way involved in the ill-fortune that has befallen him and his family. And, in truth, such action on your part would do no good. You would place yourself at risk to no purpose."

"I care not for my own peril, my lord."

"Then I beg you have a care for Lord Thomas's wishes – you can do naught else for him."

"How can I be sure of that, papa?"

"By accepting the fact that Lord Thomas and I are of one mind on the subject," said Lord Dorset. "Distressing as it is for you – indeed for all of us – the matter must take its course."

"But you fail to understand," Catherine said tearfully. "Thomas Howard is the most kind, handsome and attractive gentleman in the whole world. How can I stand by and let him die without lifting so much as a finger to save him?"

"Only the King can save him."

"Then grant me permission to go to the King."

"You would do no good, daughter, believe me." Lord Dorset hesitated for a moment, as if debating the wisdom of his next words. "Also, in granting you such permission, I would be acting contrary to what could well be Lord Thomas's last request."

"How so, my lord?"

"I will read you the last part of his letter," said Lord Dorset. "The first part concerns your removal from Kenninghall."

As he unfolded the letter and started to read, Catherine listened intently.

"A mutual regard has grown up between Lady Catherine and myself, the knowledge of which is my greatest joy and comfort during these dark days.

"It occurs to me that Lady Catherine may express a desire to come to London, to plead for me with His Majesty, or to seek permission to visit me. Neither would be to any purpose. The Countess of Surrey, my brother's wife, has besought the Privy Council to grant her an audience with His Majesty and to permit her to see her husband. Her requests have been firmly refused. I beg therefore, my lord, that you will use every means in your power to prevent Lady Catherine doing likewise. No good – but perhaps harm – would come of it.

"There is still the possibility of my being reprieved. But so faint is the possibility that I leave it solely to your discretion, my lord, as to whether or not it would be wise to give Lady Catherine a small glimmer of hope.

"My lord father and I are housed in separate chambers here in the Tower and, due to our rank, are permitted to have our own servants in attendance. I have therefore arranged that, as soon as my fate has been sealed on 27th January and my execution is a *fait accompli,* my trusted manservant, Colbran, will ride forthwith to Sackville Hall to inform you of the news and deliver a letter from me to Lady Catherine."

"May Our Lord keep you and yours in his blessed protection."

"BINDON"

*"Written in the Tower of London
on this fourteenth day of
December 1546"*

"Thomas Howard, Viscount Bindon to the Earl of Dorset."

Twenty

The days that followed Catherine's return to Sackville Hall passed with agonising slowness for her.

During her stay at Kenninghall, her family had gradually become accustomed to her absence. They loved her dearly and their joy at the reunion was genuine enough but, if Catherine seemed a little remote and abstracted now, they were not as concerned as they might formerly have been.

Catherine had gone away, albeit with reluctance, to marry a stranger. She had returned some two months later, only to discover that the stranger was after all likely to remain a stranger, since a few weeks hence he had a rendezvous with the executioner.

Catherine will get over it! her sisters said to themselves with the easy optimism of the young. A new match can easily be arranged. Catherine is pretty, very pretty, and she is usually happy and serene. At present she is sad. Viscount Bindon is very handsome, Brigid says, and Catherine has fallen in love with him. And now that they are separated, she is unhappy and love-lorn. Perchance she is dramatizing the situation, and likes to see herself as a tragically bereaved bride-to-be. After all, Viscount Bindon can still be little more than a stranger for, by all accounts, he was much away from home whilst Catherine was at Kenninghall. In truth she has known him for only a few weeks. Dear Catherine! 'Tis best to leave her alone. Then she will soon come round and it will be as if she had never gone away.

There had been a heavy fall of snow since Catherine's return and it was plain it would be a white Christmas. But neither the beauty of snow-blanketed gardens or frost-spangled trees, nor the Christmas festivities, helped to lighten Catherine's spirits. Disregarding the pleas of her sisters to join them in the gardens for a game of snowballs, she remained in her chamber.

Her thoughts were ever with her betrothed. Can he see the snow through the narrow, iron-grilled window of his prison cell? she wondered. Does the knowledge that it is Christmas increase his anguish as it does mine? Can he think back to the joys of past Christmases, and accept the fact that it is unlikely he will see another?

She drew comfort from the companionship of Lucy, who had been closely associated with the Howards and Kenninghall all her life, and was homesick for her native Norfolk.

James's presence too was a consolation to her, and seemed in some curious way to bring her closer to his father. He had settled down happily in the Sackville household and already he and Richard were boon companions, although some quite trivial happening would remind him of his mother and Catherine would subsequently find him in his bedchamber weeping piteously.

It had been decided to keep from James the knowledge of his father's peril for the time being, and neither he nor Richard were aware that anything was wrong. James had been told only that, as it was expected that his father would be detained in London for several weeks more, Catherine had decided to pay a visit to her family home.

Brigid, who was now happily married to her woodcutter, came to visit Catherine and pass judgement on her new maid.

"A bit young, isn't she?" was her summing up.

"She is near my own age and we get on well together," Catherine told her.

Brigid sniffed disapprovingly. "Too much of a chatterbox, I'd say – still, there's no accounting for tastes! I trust she's taken proper care of you. You look thinner, lovey – didn't they feed you properly in Norfolk? Foreign food needs a bit of getting used to of course ..."

"It has nothing to do with the food, Brigid," sighed

Catherine. "I have had much on my mind of late."

"I'm not surprised!" said Brigid tartly. "I'd like to give Viscount Bindon a piece of my mind. The cheek of it! Fancy foisting his bastard on …"

"That will do, Brigid," Catherine said with unwonted sharpness. "It is none of your business, and Master James is very dear to me."

Brigid gave her a long, shrewd stare. "If I believed that, I'd believe anything. By my faith, 'twould not be natural! Still, as you say, it's none of my business. You've changed, my lady. You look like one who's forgotten how to smile – and you only in your sixteenth winter!"

"There is little to smile about, Brigid," said Catherine.

"'Twas a pity you ever took off to that there Kenninghall – I always thought it," said Brigid. "I knew you'd not be happy in a household run by that Jezebel …"

"Bess Holland has nothing to do with my unhappiness," insisted Catherine. "Well, not in the way you mean anyway. So long as my lord Thomas was there at Kenninghall …"

She dissolved into tears at that point and Brigid patted her hand consolingly.

"Don't fret so, lovey," she said. "Your betrothed lord is not dead yet …"

Catherine's tears turned into sobs at this and Brigid looked a trifle put out. Even she, it seemed, regarded Catherine's tragedy as no more than a passing sorrow.

"There, there, lovey! You don't approve of my plain speaking – is that it?" asked Brigid cheerfully. "You never minded it before. Anyway, I've got some good news for you …"

"Good news?" asked Catherine on a hopeful note.

"'Twill brighten you up and give you something else to think about!"

"There is only one item of news that would brighten my spirits," Catherine said tearfully, "and clearly 'tis not that you are about to tell me."

"Life has to go on, lovey," Brigid pointed out. "You wait till you hear my news – you'll be the first to know. I am with child – now what do you think of that?"

"It – is – wonderful – news," sobbed Catherine. "I – am – so – glad – Brigid."

"You sound it, I must say!" said Brigid huffily. "I hope it won't have the same effect on my husband when I tell him."

"My lady is a little upset at present," explained Lucy, entering the chamber at that moment.

"Is she now? Thank you for telling me, lass – I'd never have guessed," Brigid said tartly.

"She's not been herself lately," persisted Lucy.

"Well, if she's not herself, then perchance you can tell me who she is," said Brigid roundly. "Has she been bewitched or something? Or is it that you're not taking proper care of her? She was never like this when I looked after her! Of course, you are a Norfolk lass …"

Reminded suddenly of home, Lucy too dissolved into tears at this point, and Brigid gazed from mistress to maidservant and back again in astonishment.

"By me grandaddy's bones!" she exclaimed. "I'd best be on me way before I get drowned in the flood! If the news that I'm with child is going to have this effect on everybody, I'll tell my husband he must needs get busy building us an ark!"

"Oh – Brigid – please – forgive – me," said Catherine, her words punctuated by sobs. "'Tis – just – that – when – you – told – me – it – reminded – me – of …"

But already Brigid was fleeing the chamber.

*   *   *

Only Lord Dorset fully understood his daughter's anguish. He knew what she was suffering, but recognized that there was nothing he or any of his family could do to assuage her grief.

Catherine is like me, Heaven help her, he thought to himself. She is a Sackville through and through. She will love truly but once in her lifetime. Would that I had not sent her to Norfolk! Would that she had not set eyes on young Howard! I recall how she pleaded not to go. But the harm is done, alas!

It was like that with me when my beloved wife died, he thought. She was sixteen, like Catherine, when I married her.

We were all but strangers when she became my bride, and I sensed her shyness and her doubts, but from that time forth we were all in all to each other. Time heals, it is said. Maybe it does – for some. For others, the loss of one's beloved remains an open wound that causes pain for the rest of one's life, and from which only death offers release. One longs at times for death, feeling that, even if reunion with one's beloved is denied, peace and oblivion would be infinitely preferable to the pain of living.

But since we have a duty to the living, and others are dependent on us, life has to go on, whether we will or nay. After a while, one learns to live with one's wound and to take each day as it comes …

Lord Dorset pulled himself together. Why am I sitting here thus, lost in reverie? he thought to himself. Why am I harking back to the past when the present – and perchance the future – is clamouring for my attention?

Four weeks have elapsed since Catherine's return. A new year has been born and is now twenty-one days old.

This morning I received information from my own sources in London. Now I must summon Catherine and tell her what has befallen.

Still she hopes – I sense it. Perchance this latest happening will prepare her for the worst. Please God she will accept the fact that there is no hope of a reprieve for the man she loves; that, since the King signed the death warrant of his favourite, he will certainly not balk at spilling the blood of his favourite's father and brother.

* * *

"You wished to speak to me, my lord?" asked Catherine, trying to quell the agitation that had afflicted her ever since she had received his summons.

"Yes, my dear," said Lord Dorset. "Pray be seated. I fear that what I am about to tell you will but increase your distress, but it would be unwise to withhold the information from you, alas."

"There is news from London?" she asked in a small, anxious voice.

"There is indeed, my daughter. Ever since I learned of the Earl of Surrey's arrest, I have as you know retained a trusted messenger in London. He keeps an ear to the ground and reports to me whenever he has fresh information."

"And he has fresh information, papa?"

Lord Dorset's expression was grave. "I regret to inform you that the Earl of Surrey was beheaded on Tower Hill yesterday morning, the 20th January."

"That was to have been my wedding day, papa," Catherine said, with seeming inconsequence. "My lord of Surrey was to have been Best Man."

"Pray do not dwell on that now, my child," urged Lord Dorset. "You will only distress yourself the more."

Catherine's eyes filled with tears. "It matters not about my distress, papa. 'Tis poor Frances who concerns me. How will she live with the anguish? Did the King relent – before the end?"

"Relent?" asked Lord Dorset, not understanding the question. "But I just told you ..."

"I meant was Frances permitted to see her husband before his execution?" interposed Catherine.

Lord Dorset shook his head. "Nay, she did not set eyes on him after that day, many weeks ago, when he departed in complete confidence from Mount Surrey – so I am informed."

"Alas, papa, it is all too dreadful! Henry of Surrey was such a gallant gentleman," sighed Catherine. "He was full of life and enthusiasm – and his reputation as a poet has given him a romantic image."

"His poems at least will be a fitting memorial for him," said Lord Dorset. "I fear there will be no other."

"He was only in his twenty-ninth year, papa, but he had served His Majesty faithfully and to good purpose."

"He died bravely, I am told."

"Knowing him, one could not imagine otherwise," said Catherine tremulously.

"During the final days of his imprisonment, he was given to alternating moods, I understand: fury against his enemies who had brought him and his family to such a pass, and anxiety for his wife and children."

"That he and Frances were denied the opportunity of saying farewell is beyond belief," declared Catherine.

"He was permitted to write a farewell letter to her, it seems," Lord Dorset told her. "And to receive the Blessed Sacrament on the morning of his execution."

"How could the King have let him die, papa? Surrey was innocent of treason – I know he was!"

"He declared as much from the scaffold," Lord Dorset said. "He condemned the wicked and evil knaves who had destroyed him. He died, fortified by the rites of Holy Church, and with Lady Frances's name on his lips."

"My lord, I realize why you are telling me all this," Catherine said white-faced. "You wish to prepare me for the knowledge that all hope of a reprieve for my lord Thomas is lost. Is it not so?"

"It is, my daughter," nodded Lord Dorset. "Would that I could tell you otherwise!"

"Is there no justice left in England, papa?" demanded Catherine. "First Surrey, and then ..."

Her voice broke, and Lord Dorset shook his head sorrowfully.

"Surrey was indeed innocent of treason – I am convinced of that," he said. "But he refused to temper his hatred of his enemies with expediency – he thereby gave them the means to destroy him."

"In truth, papa, I could more easily believe the Duke of Norfolk guilty of high treason than either of his sons," admitted Catherine. "Though he treated me always with kindness and courtesy."

"The Duke is cunning and ruthless, one who keeps his thoughts and intentions well hidden until he sees the auspicious moment to strike against his enemies," Lord Dorset told her. "All his life he has played a dangerous game skilfully. Now, thanks to Surrey's rashness, he has been beaten at his own game and is to die in his seventy-third year. He has had a good innings!"

"But Lord Thomas has played no part in political intrigues,

papa," pointed out Catherine. "He preferred the life of a country squire, and acted as overseer of the Howard estates during his father's frequent absences. He is known to everyone who lives or works on the estates, be they farmer or peasant. He has no enemies – I feel sure of that."

"Any man who has power or wealth – albeit he uses his assets for the benefit of his fellows – has enemies. That is a fact of life, my daughter," Lord Dorset told her grimly. "As son to England's premier duke, Thomas Howard was born with enemies. One cannot escape one's destiny, alas."

"Is not it an ill-omen, papa, that my lord of Surrey should have been executed on what was to have been my bridal day?" asked Catherine, with a catch in her voice.

"An ill-omen? I know not. Who can tell what the future holds for any of us?"

"Then …?"

"I fear you must prepare yourself for the worst," Lord Dorset said firmly. "Believe me, I understand your distress only too well, and know how deeply you are suffering at the present time. You are young, some would say, and will soon overcome your grief! But the number of one's years bears no relation to the depth of one's sorrow at the loss of one's beloved – I am convinced of that. I would be doing you an ill-service in offering you hope when, God have pity, there looks to be none."

"I will try to prepare myself for the worst, as you say, papa," Catherine said tearfully. "If only I did not love him so! If only I could have seen him, or received some personal message from him!"

"There is a message from him – a letter addressed to myself," said Lord Dorset then, in sudden decision. "I was undecided as to the wisdom of mentioning it."

"Pray tell me of it, papa."

"My messenger in London arranged for a note to be conveyed to Lord Thomas yesterday by means of His Lordship's servants," explained Lord Dorset. "A brief letter from His Lordship addressed to myself was smuggled out of the Tower and brought here to me this morning."

"May I read it, papa?" pleaded Catherine.

Lord Dorset took the letter from a drawer in his writing desk and handed it to her.

"Pray do so, child," he said. "It is brief and to the point. There was danger to all concerned in conveying such a message secretly from the Tower – His Lordship's letters are customarily intercepted, needless to say – and the matter was conducted in some haste."

Blinking back the tears that misted her eyes as she unfolded the letter and saw Lord Thomas's handwriting, Catherine started to read:

"My lord,

Since learning of my brother's death this morning, I am persuaded that hope of a reprieve for my lord father and myself can no longer be entertained.

My man, Colbran, will set forth for Sackville Hall immediately after my execution on 27th January in order to inform you of the fact, and to convey to Lady Catherine a farewell letter which I shall previously entrust to him.

If through some miracle, my life should be spared, I myself shall ride to Sackville Hall to claim my bride."

"BINDON"

"Written in the Tower of London
on this twentieth day of
January 1547"

"Thomas Howard, Viscount Bindon to the Earl of Dorset."

Twenty-One

The day that Catherine had been dreading, that was to set the seal on her hopes, dawned bright and fair. The golden sun-kissed morning of 28th January 1547 was unusually beautiful for the time of year and, combining with the joyful chorus of the birds, seemed to mock her unhappiness.

She remained in her chamber all the morning, seeing no one but her father and Lucy, and refusing the food that was brought to her.

Her sisters had undertaken to look after James and keep him and Richard amused, and for that Catherine was grateful. James would thus be spared the realization of her distress – for the time being.

When will the news come? she asked herself over and over again. Yesterday saw the end of my hopes of happiness – despite father's warning, I had till then never entirely abandoned hope. Today, Colbran, my lord's messenger, should be coming here, to tell us of his master's last moments and bearing his farewell letter to me. By fast riding and a frequent change of horses, the journey could be accomplished by this afternoon, father told me.

Hope is gone, but still I long for news. What did my lord say to me in his farewell letter? Were his last thoughts of me as he placed his head upon the block? I know he would have died bravely, but I wish to hear at first-hand of those last precious moments of his life. Since he is now dead …

Dead? she thought. Contrary to reason and commonsense and in spite of father's warning – I believe dear papa is the only one who truly understands how I feel – still in my innermost being I cannot accept that he whom I love is dead. Would not my heart tell me if he were dead? Would not I feel it in my very bones if I were not to see him again? My heart does not speak so, and I cannot believe I shall never see him again …

Alas, why do I torment myself thus? Catherine asked herself. Is it because I am unable to face the truth?

My lord and I had known each other, discovered our love for each other, for so pitifully short a time. He needed me. I realise that now. In all his life, it was only I who learned in our short time together to understand him, and love him simply for being himself. I cannot help but think of what might have been. Eight days ago, I was to have become his bride. How I had longed for that day, and the night that would have followed and made me truly his …

It was at that point in Catherine's reverie that Lucy entered the chamber.

"Shall I draw back the curtains, my lady?" she asked. "'Tis such a beautiful day."

"So was yesterday!" Catherine said, bitterly. "So was yesterday – the day they killed my lord!"

"I'll draw back the curtains just the same, my lady. The sunshine will do you good," said Lucy firmly, going over to the window. "Your lord father wishes to see you in his library as soon as possible."

Catherine's heart gave a sudden leap. "The messenger has arrived?" she asked agitatedly.

"I know not, my lady. His lordship just said: 'Tell Lady Catherine I wish to see her in my library as soon as possible.'" Lucy smiled. "Anyway, you surely don't want to be seen looking like that, do you?"

"Like what?"

"With a tear-stained face, a crumpled gown, and your hair all mussed as if a pair of swallows have built a nest in it!"

"I care not how I look," retorted Catherine. "Why should I care? Would father, knowing how I feel, expect to see me looking happy and smiling and wearing my best gown?"

"His Lordship would expect you to keep up appearances, my lady, however you felt inside," Lucy said forthrightly. "You don't need me to tell you that."

"His Lordship?"

"Your lord father," said Lucy hastily.

"I thought for one moment you were making reference to my betrothed lord." Catherine's eyes brimmed with fresh tears. "You were, were you not?"

Lucy nodded but said nothing, busying herself with pouring warm water into the hand-basin and fetching fresh ribbons and underclothes for her mistress.

"You were right, Lucy. You did need to remind me," Catherine admitted. "My lord Thomas would have wished me to receive the formal affirmation of his death with the composure and dignity befitting a lady, the bride-to-be of a Howard."

"Shall I fetch your black silk gown, my lady?"

"Yes, that will be suitable," Catherine said carelessly, but then she hesitated. "Wait, though. Perchance ... Nay, Lucy, not the black. I shall wear the jade green."

"Green, my lady? But green is ..."

"Unlucky?" Catherine's tone was rueful. "Indeed you were right there also. Perchance I should have paid heed to your warning. But it is too late for that now!"

"My lady, I was about to say that the green gown is unsuitable – in the circumstances."

"And that is where you are wrong, Lucy! 'Tis eminently suitable – nothing could be more suitable," insisted Catherine. "'Tis the gown I was wearing when my lord and I first met. My lady Greensleeves he called me to himself then – though I did not discover that till later. Then again, at our farewell, I was robed in green – it was as if I had guessed that he was to give me the emerald pendant as a parting gift. What then could be more suitable, on the occasion when I am to receive corroboration of his death, than my green gown – and the emerald pendant?"

"You will wear the emerald pendant also?" asked Lucy in surprise. "But my lady, only jet or gold jewellery is considered suitable for one in mourning. Surely ..."

"I shall wear the emerald pendant – I have made up my mind."

"As you will, my lady," Lucy's voice made plain her disapproval. "Though I doubt whether your lord father – or the messenger if he has arrived – will approve your choice."

But already she had helped to remove Catherine's crumpled gown, and was adding rose-water to the water already in the basin in order to bathe her young mistress's tear-stained face.

"You know, Lucy, it is hard to believe that I knew my lord Thomas for so brief a time," mused Catherine, as Lucy started to dress her. "I feel as if I have known him all my life."

"You look truly beautiful, my lady," said Lucy, standing back to survey her handiwork and deciding it would be wise to refrain from commenting on Catherine's last remark. "You are all ready now to answer your lord father's summons. You look a trifle pale, it must be admitted, but no one would guess that – that ..."

As she floundered for the right words, Catherine completed the sentence for her.

"That my heart has died?" she asked quietly. "I look well enough, thanks to you – I would like to think that my lord would have been proud of me."

As she went from the chamber to make her way to the library, Lucy gazed after her, her own eyes brimming with tears.

"Poor lass!" she said softly. "'Twas an ill day for her, the day she set forth for Norfolk. 'Twas the wearing of the green that did it of course – I knew no good would come of it and I gave her fair warning. All the same, I never dreamed it would turn out like this."

Twenty-Two

As Catherine neared the library, her pace slackened – as if even now she sought to put off for as long as possible the moment when she would hear the truth.

Papa is waiting for me, she thought. And I expect Colbran, my lord Thomas's messenger, is with him. I told papa that I myself wished to see Colbran, that I might question him as to my lord's last moments.

I must remain calm, she told herself as she reached the library door. My heart is weeping, and already tears are welling up into my eyes at the thought of what lies ahead.

I shall wait here in the passageway for a few moments and then, once I have regained my composure, I shall make my entrance.

She smoothed her already immaculately dressed hair, straightened the folds of the green gown, and ran her fingers over the emerald pendant that lay against her white throat – as if to draw courage from its cold beauty. Then, with sudden resolve, she knocked on the door and went into the library.

But even as she crossed the threshold, her eyes misted with tears, so that she looked unseeingly at the tall figure who stood, his back towards her, in front of the fireplace.

"Papa?" she asked tremulously.

The figure turned to face her at the very same instant that she blinked away her tears. She saw that he was smiling at her. That he was holding out his arms to her.

She stared in disbelief.

"My lord Thomas?" she murmured then, incredulously. "Is it you? Nay, it cannot be. I am bemused by grief. It cannot be – it cannot ..."

In a few rapid strides he had crossed the space that separated them and was drawing her into his arms. He looked tenderly down at her.

"It is I, beloved," he said.

She gazed up at him breathlessly, mistrusting the evidence of her eyes, while tears ran unheeded down her cheeks and on to the green gown.

"Nay, 'tis not possible," she whispered.

"Do not weep, beloved," he said. "We are here together – the time for weeping is past."

"I still cannot believe it," she said softly. "I fear I must be dreaming."

"And still you weep," he smiled. "Does my arrival cause you so much sorrow?"

She reached up then, and clasped her arms around his neck in fierce protection, thus answering his question.

"But I do not understand," she murmured. "Why are you here, my lord? Could it be that you have been permitted to come here to bid me farewell – has the King granted us that one favour?"

"King Henry is no longer able to either bestow or withhold favours," Lord Thomas said grimly. "At four o'clock yesterday morning, 27th January – the very morning on which my lord father and I were to have been executed – King Henry died in his sleep."

"Mother of mercy!" exclaimed Catherine. "Can it be true?"

He nodded, watching her changing expression tenderly.

"Then God does answer prayers," she said softly. "I prayed and prayed that something would happen to save you, that some miracle would prevent your execution. I never dreamed that my prayers would be answered thus. I knew that King Henry was ailing, but he had been in poor health for many months, had he not?"

"His death was indeed opportune for my father and myself," Lord Thomas said sombrely. "Alas that it came too late to save my brother! Henry of Surrey, may he rest in peace, did not deserve to die."

"I know that, my lord. I was grief-stricken when I learned of his fate," Catherine told him. "I wished to go to poor Frances, but my father forbade it."

"His Lordship was right, sweeting. Frances and her children are now under the protection of her father, the Earl of Oxford. Frances is near her time – the birth is expected in three weeks, I understand. My brother's last child will be posthumous, alas!"

"Then Frances and the children have left Mount Surrey?"

Lord Thomas nodded gravely. "Mount Surrey was sacked, I am told, by order of the Seymours, and is now an empty shell," he said.

"That beautiful house! Your brother and Frances regarded it as their first real home and it was the scene of much happiness. 'Tis all so dreadful!" It was then that a new and disquieting thought struck Catherine. "And what of you, my lord? Have you been pardoned? Or will you be required to undergo another trial now that there is a new monarch?"

"The order of execution has been rescinded," he told her. "King Henry has been succeeded by his son Edward, and the new King's advisers considered it would be an ill-omen if the new reign were to commence with an act of bloodshed."

"Then you are free, my lord?" asked Catherine joyously. "Really and truly free?"

He smiled, savouring her joy. "Really and truly," he nodded. "My father will remain a prisoner in the Tower for the time being, but his life has been spared, God be praised."

"Still I can scarcely believe it. My father knows of course?"

"It was he who suggested leaving us alone, so that I could speak for myself." Lord Thomas smiled wickedly. "He even went so far as to hint that you, my lady, had been pining for me."

"Indeed I did pine for you – I freely admit it. My life seemed empty and without hope – it was as if my heart had died and my body, like Mount Surrey, was an empty shell! Alas, my lord, I knew I loved you, but I never realized just how much until methought I had lost you for ever."

"Then I had the advantage of you, my lady," he said

earnestly. "I knew I loved you, in a way that I would never love another, from the first moment I set eyes on you – my lady Greensleeves."

"Let me look at you, my lord," she said, standing back to gaze lovingly at him. "Let me feast my eyes upon you – even now I feel that you are but a mirage and that you will suddenly disappear before my very eyes."

In mourning for his beloved brother, Lord Thomas was dressed in black, his velvet doublet and hose being without embellishment of any kind. But the sombre apparel gave emphasis to the shining beauty of his dark eyes, Catherine noticed, and to the heavy gold chain which held a crucifix of solid gold, set with four blood-red rubies that represented the nails that pierced the hands and feet of Christ crucified.

"My lady Greensleeves, you called me just now," she said. "Perchance, though I was unaware of it at the time, I had an intuition when I donned this gown today."

He nodded. "It will be your bridal gown," he said.

"My bridal gown? Nay, I would not wish ..."

"I discussed the matter with your lord father before he summoned you here," he told her, "and he and I are of one mind in the matter ..."

"My father wishes me to wear this green gown instead of the bridal white that has been made ready for me? Is that what you would have me believe?" Catherine smiled. "You are surely teasing me, my lord!"

"The colour of your bridal gown was not the subject of the discussion between your father and myself," Lord Thomas said quietly. "It was the bridal itself of which we spoke."

"Indeed, my lord?"

"Our marriage was lawfully contracted thirteen years ago, beloved. We have yet to be married in accordance with the rite of Holy Church. Only then can I make you truly mine."

"I am aware of that, my lord."

"In a few hours' time we shall be married by a Catholic priest in the private chapel here at Sackville," he told her. "It will be a quiet wedding, with naught but your family and members of the household to act as witnesses."

"What of your family, my lord?" she asked softly.

"My family?" His voice was sorrowful. "Alas that Henry of Surrey, and Frances, and my lord father will not, cannot, be there!"

"Your son will be there, my lord," Catherine said quietly.

"My son?" he asked in surprise. "My son? To whom are you referring?"

"How many sons have you, my lord, that you should ask such a question?" enquired Catherine with mock severity. "Have there been other peccadilloes?"

"There is only James, my bastard, but he ..."

"...is here at Sackville," Catherine finished for him.

"Here at Sackville?" he asked incredulously. "My lady, this is no subject for levity. I love my son dearly."

"I too love him dearly, my lord."

"You? But how ...? I do not understand."

"My lord, I will explain later how it was that James became my protégé." Her eyes were suddenly bright with tears, he noticed. "Suffice it for the present to tell you that he is indeed here at Sackville – as oblivious of your arrival as I was! Oh, how I have longed and prayed for your reunion! Now that all my prayers have been answered, I must be the happiest maiden in the whole world!"

"Alas, that your happiness must be short-lived!" remarked Lord Thomas.

"Short-lived?" Catherine looked startled. "What mean you, my lord?"

He drew her into his arms and looked tenderly down at her upturned face. His voice when he spoke was deep with emotion.

"When tonight is past, you will be a maiden no longer – have you given thought to that?" he asked.

Her smile was sweet and shy and gentle – just as a maiden's should be! But her voice was warm and loving and full of promise – and belied the innocence of her smile.

"I am giving thought to it, my lord," she said.